Health Care

Health Care

Look for these and other books in the Lucent Overview Series:

Health Care

by Deborah S. Romaine

Lucent
Books

LUCENT Overview Series

Library of Congress Cataloging-in-Publication Data

Romaine, Deborah S., 1956–
    Health care / by Deborah S. Romaine.
        p.   cm. — (Lucent overview series)
    Includes bibliographical references and index.
    Summary: Discusses various aspects of modern health care,
including the changing profession of medicine, access to health care
services, keeping communities healthy, health care costs, ethics, and
the future.
    ISBN 1-56006-488-9 (lib. bdg. : alk. paper)
    1. Medicine—Juvenile literature.   2. Health—Juvenile literature.
3. Medical ethics—Juvenile literature.   4. Medical care—Juvenile
literature. [1. Medical care. 2. Medicine.]   I. Title.   II. Series.
R130.5.R66   2000
362.1—dc21
                                                          99-36999
                                                            CIP

Copyright © 2000 by Lucent Books, Inc.
P.O. Box 289011, San Diego, CA 92198-9011
Printed in the U.S.A.

Contents

Introduction

-THE UNITED STATES boasts the most advanced medical care in the world. American physicians routinely transplant organs and create babies in test tubes and are more successful at treating cancer and other serious illnesses than physicians in any other nation. Wealthy foreigners often seek treatment in the United States, knowing that they will receive the best medicine money can buy.

-Most Americans receive adequate, even excellent, health care in this system. These are the insured Americans—those whose companies provide health care benefits or those who can afford private health care policies. These citizens often receive preventive care through regular examinations and they feel confident that, should they become seriously ill, they will be treated and the bulk of the costs will be covered by insurance.-

-Unfortunately, more than 37 million Americans remain uninsured. They may be employees of the one-fourth of companies that do not provide health care coverage. They may be uninsurable because of a previous medical condition. Or they may be unemployed and too poor to afford private health insurance but not poor enough to qualify for government assistance.

-Most of the uninsured cannot afford preventive care such as physical examinations and treatment for minor illnesses. And when their untreated minor illnesses develop into major ones, many of these Americans seek treatment in hospital emergency rooms, where the care may be good but the cost is extremely high for the hospital. When patients cannot pay for this care, hospitals either absorb the cost or it gets passed on to other, paying patients in the form of higher insurance premiums, hospital room rates, and physicians' fees. Some hospitals have even begun turning away uninsured patients to avoid the cost of treating them.

This is the plight of the uninsured. But even insured Americans are not guaranteed complete financial coverage of their medical treatment. Many, when faced with a severe illness, find that their insurance is inadequate or that their insurance company is no longer willing to insure them. For example, eight-year-old Marisa Harvey of Leucadia, California, had only one kidney, which did not fully function. After doctors discovered her problem when she was three, her family's insurance company began doubling their health insurance premium every year. After five years, the family was paying $16,000 annually in health care premiums. They could not afford the price hikes and lost their insurance.

Situations like the Harveys' were once unusual, but now are becoming more common. This is largely because many

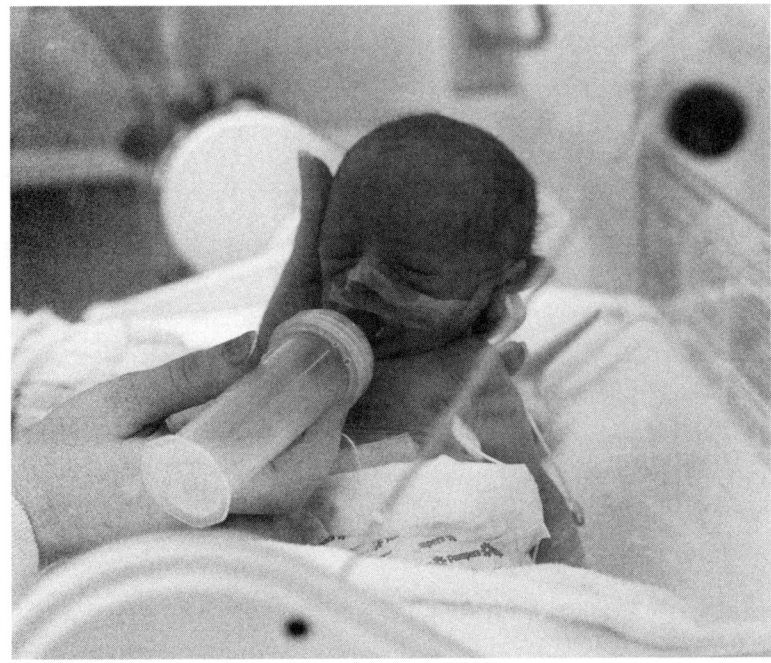

Test-tube babies are a testament to the advanced medical care of the United States.

President Clinton's plan for reforming the health care system failed to win congressional support.

insurance companies are changing their business practices: To compete with other companies for customers, companies increasingly are separating the healthy from the sick, and offering the healthy lower premiums. The sick, meanwhile, face soaring rates and reduced coverage. Because of these changes, thousands of Americans, suffering under the expense of treating a serious illness or paying exorbitantly high premiums, have been financially devastated. And the healthy face the prospect of high premiums should they become sick.

Millions of Americans are affected by the gaps in America's health care coverage. But fixing these gaps alone will not solve the nation's health care problems. America must also address rising health care costs and the fact that the overall price the nation pays for health care is already the highest in the world.

Excessive spending on health care burdens the nation's economy by siphoning money and resources away from other problems that call for attention. It also impedes economic growth.

Nearly all Americans agree that escalating health care costs must be controlled, but they disagree on how to control them. A variety of plans have been proposed, from minor reforms to the revamping of the entire system. President Bill Clinton in September 1993 proposed a plan that he believed would guarantee health insurance coverage for all Americans while controlling costs and providing good health care. His critics lambasted the plan, arguing that it was too complicated and would be prohibitively expensive.

Whether they supported or opposed Clinton's health care policies and other ideas offered since that time, most Americans would agree that the health care system is in need of reform. Deciding how best to reform that system remains a key challenge for public policymakers both now and in the future.

1

Managing Health Care

⌐AMERICA'S HEALTH CARE costs are rising. Spending on health care surpassed $1 trillion in 1996, making health care the country's single largest expense. The huge cost increases that have contributed to this sum make it difficult to provide quality health care services to everyone who needs them. This situation has led to changes in how health care services are provided.⌐The most common form of health care delivery today is managed care, a system of monitoring and managing health care services, providers, and costs. The intent of managed care is to deliver the broadest array of health care services to the greatest number of people in the most efficient ways.

Efforts to achieve this balance have had mixed results. Most experts believe that managed care plans have successfully controlled costs while providing quality care for large numbers of people. Managed care has also been the focus of critics who say it limits choice for patients and restricts the decisions doctors make about testing and treatment. These critics worry that efforts to deal with the rising costs of health care services have overshadowed concerns about the quality of those services.

Although experts debate about how to bring health care costs down, they agree that rising costs threaten the availability of health care services for the general population. In 1950, for example, a typical visit to a doctor cost around five dollars. Today, that same visit would cost at least eighty-five

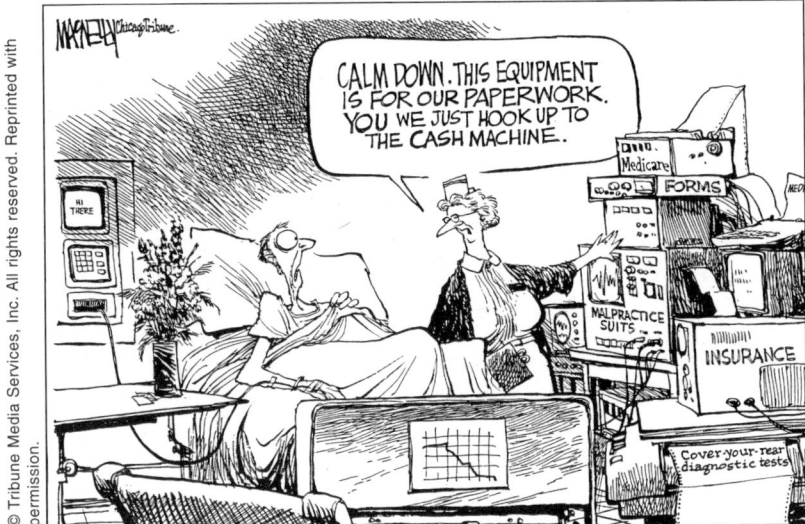

dollars. While the costs of other services and products have also risen over time, health care costs have increased at a much faster rate. Many reasons have been suggested for the rise in health care costs.

Expensive expectations

An explosion of new technology is one reason for the rising costs. Advances in medical technology have made modern medicine more effective. CT (computerized tomography) scans and MRI (magnetic resonance imaging) procedures, for example, make it possible to "see" inside the body without surgery. These sophisticated technologies can detect many conditions, from cancers to strokes, in their earliest stages. This makes it possible to start treatment before the condition causes serious or irreversible damage, saving thousands of lives every year.

Other notable advances have been in surgery, where highly skilled specialists can repair or even replace organs and body parts damaged by disease or injury. Lasers and fiber optics have made great contributions to surgery, often permitting surgeons to use very

Magnetic resonance imaging (MRI) enables doctors to see inside the body without performing surgery.

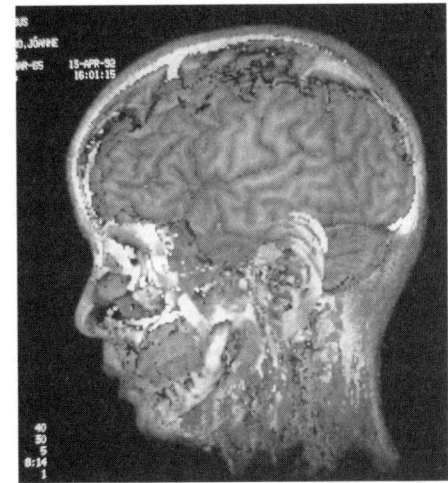

small incisions to get instruments deep into the body. Such minimally invasive procedures allow patients to heal far more quickly than did the old method of making large incisions to expose internal organs.

The successes of technology do not come cheap, though. Sophisticated procedures cost hundreds or even thousands of dollars each time they are used. They require special facilities and highly trained staff. As just one example, nearly twenty-five hundred Americans receive heart transplants each year at a cost of more than two hundred thouand dollars each. It also costs around fifteen thousand dollars a year for the rest of the person's life for medications and ongoing care.

Among the most significant advances in medical technology are those in drugs, or pharmaceuticals. Drugs improve or extend the lives of hundreds of thousands of people every year, from infants to the elderly. New discoveries lead to new kinds of drugs that not only treat but also can prevent certain diseases. "In the pharmaceutical industry, technological advances used to occur once every twenty-four months," write C. Duane Dauner and Michael Bowker in their book *The Health Care Solution: Understanding the Crisis and the Cure.* "Today, one occurs every twenty-four hours."[1] The cost of developing new drugs is high. Americans already spend billions of dollars each year on prescription medications, and that amount is likely to climb with continuing advances.

Huge demand for new technology and new drugs also keeps health care costs high. An aging population is one significant factor in this equation. Those who study population trends project that the number of Americans over age sixty-five will double from 32.5 million in 1999 to 65 million by the year 2030, making this age group one-fourth of the country's population. People who live longer have more—and more serious—health care needs. This means the demand for medical technology keeps growing. The combination of new technologies and an increasing demand for them further increases health care costs.

Inefficient practices

Experts also cite waste and inefficiency in the practice of medicine as partly to blame for health care's high costs. Doctors have numerous choices when it comes to ordering tests and prescribing treatments. They typically order enough tests to identify the cause of a patient's symptoms and determine an appropriate course of treatment. But some doctors go beyond what is strictly necessary, ordering tests that may not be helpful. In some cases, they do this to protect themselves from possible lawsuits. With lawsuits returning record judgments against hospitals, clinics, and doctors, many doctors feel compelled to order extra tests to avoid claims that they missed a diagnosis.

In their book, Dauner and Bowker underscore the magnitude of the problem:

> Unnecessary medical procedures cost American consumers nearly $130 billion annually. . . . Cesarean sections, hysterectomies, some coronary bypasses, magnetic resonance imaging and other imaging services, laboratory procedures, and diagnostic tests are among the most overused procedures.[2]

Overtreatment is often a problem as well. People go to the doctor and expect to leave with something to make them feel better. Many patients press for at least a prescription, and many doctors feel compelled to comply. This results in a high level of unnecessary medication and unneeded treatment. This is a difficult issue to zero in on, however. The practice of medicine relies heavily on the doctor's judgment. What is an appropriate course of treatment for one person may not fit the needs of another person, even when both have similar symptoms. One consequence of overtesting and overtreating is an increase in health care costs.

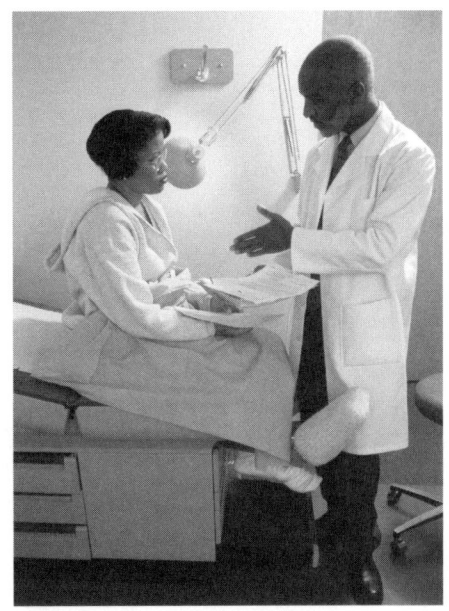

A doctor consults his patient. Some doctors prescribe unnecessary treatments in order to satisfy their patients.

The growth of managed care

Managed care is seen as a way to control costs and still provide needed health care services to a large percentage of the population. There are many forms of managed care plans. The most common of these is the health maintenance organization, or HMO. HMOs emphasize preventive care to keep people healthy and prompt intervention to keep illnesses and injuries from becoming major medical crises whenever possible. An HMO can be a network of independent community providers, including hospitals, doctors, laboratories, imaging facilities, and other health care services. Or it can operate its own hospitals and clinics and employ its own doctors, nurses, pharmacists, and other staff.

HMOs and other managed care plans provide a specific comprehensive package of health care services in return for a fixed monthly payment (often paid by an employer). Members are usually also responsible for a modest co-payment for office visits. People who choose a managed care plan must receive all medical services through the plan's providers to have the plan pay the costs. Though some managed care plans will pay a limited amount for services people receive from providers outside the plan, HMOs usually do not.

Scott Willis, San Jose Mercury News

Though managed care seems a modern answer to a current problem, it actually has its roots in the late 1940s, when few families or individuals had health insurance. Most health care was given on a fee-for-service basis, meaning a doctor or hospital charged a set rate or fee for a particular service. The patient paid the fee at the time the service was rendered. Under this system, a medical crisis could easily result in the loss of one's life savings.

Private medical insurance, available to those who could afford it, greatly lessened the risk of such loss. A yearly fee or premium entitled the insurance policyholder to coverage for major medical expenses that might result from serious illness and emergencies, but few policies covered routine care or doctor visits. Many families and individuals could not afford the cost of insurance, so they simply went without.

It was during this period that managed care got its start. Group Health Cooperative, one of the nation's first HMOs, began in 1947 in Seattle, Washington. In return for monthly or annual dues, members received comprehensive health care services (ranging from preventive care to emergency care) from designated clinics and doctors. Though other HMOs developed throughout the country in the decades that followed, this system of health care remained a small slice of the overall health care picture for many years.

Traditional medical insurance dominated through the 1970s. Experts believe this system of health coverage has contributed to the rise in health costs. People who have to pay for their own doctor visits often do not see a doctor unless the need becomes extreme. By that time, however, the cost of care may be much greater than it would have been had that person seen a doctor early. It is far more costly, for example, to perform heart surgery for clogged arteries than it is to recommend lifestyle changes and prescribe medication to reduce cholesterol levels. Yet coronary bypass surgery is the most common operation done in the United States. As family physician Mark Brooks states, "There were incentives for people to be ill, not to remain well."[3]

Costly coronary bypass surgery, often avoidable through lifestyle changes and medication, remains a common operation.

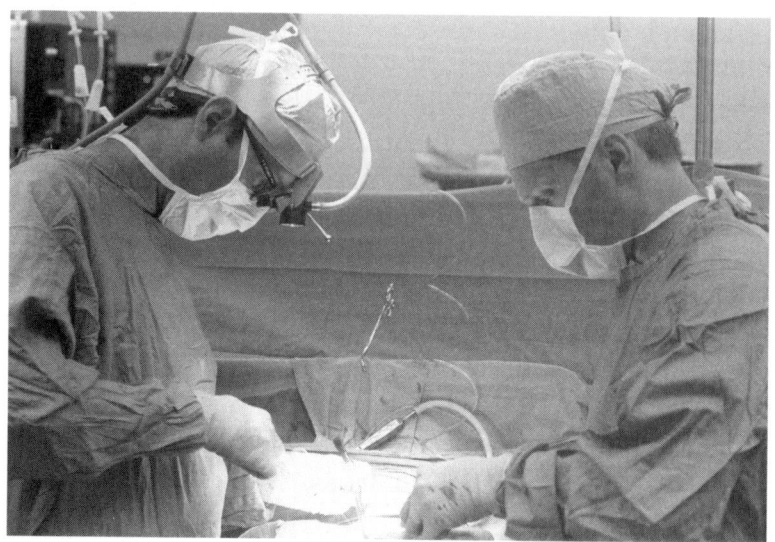

Unmet expectations

Managed care has been touted as a means of holding down costs while providing quality health care to a greater number of people. However, many people do not believe that it has achieved that goal. There is a growing level of dissatisfaction with the gap between the ideal and the reality of managed care. "Managed care evolved, as an ideal, as a means for establishing accountability," says Brooks. "The model itself is good, in that it wants to prove value based on cost and quality. I think the challenge is balancing the expectations of insurance companies, physicians, and patients."[4]

Many doctors and patients feel that managed care is failing to meet these expectations. A 1999 Harris poll reported that less than 1 percent of physicians and 6 percent of individuals questioned believed that managed care has been "very successful" in improving the quality of health care services. Nearly two-thirds of polled physicians believed that managed care was "not at all successful" in making improvements, as did 20 percent of the individuals questioned.

Satisfied patients

Others believe that managed care has succeeded despite the public perception that it has not. As one *U.S. News & World Report* writer states,

> The mounting complaints about HMOs have tended to obscure the genuine gains that have occurred in the managed-care era—for patients, for companies, for the overall economy. Thanks to managed care, most Americans have more money in their pockets and may also be healthier. Thanks to managed care, more companies can afford to provide health benefits to employees. For most Americans, however, the new system's achievements have remained largely invisible—in contrast to the highly visible indignities and inconveniences it sometimes imposes on them.[5]

Regardless of one's point of view on the success of managed care, it has gained a foothold in the American system of health care delivery. By the mid-1990s, 90 percent of American doctors were participating in some form of managed care program, and in 1999 nearly half of all patients with health insurance were enrolled in managed care plans.

Surveys show that many consumers are satisfied with their managed care providers. The American Association of Health Plans reports that surveys in 1996 and 1997 found that managed care patients were as satisfied or more satisfied with their care than were traditional fee-for-service patients. Another survey, this one done by *Consumer Reports* magazine, found that readers (representing membership in thirty-seven different HMOs) were "fairly well satisfied" to "very satisfied" with their health care providers.

Other surveys have turned up similar results. When the Xerox Corporation surveyed twenty-five thousand employees in 1994, it found that HMO members were "significantly more satisfied with their overall care than were fee-for-service patients."[6] Most of the ninety thousand federal employees surveyed in 1994 by the Federal Employees Health Benefits Program had similar views. According to that survey, 86 percent of the HMO members expressed satisfaction with their health care providers—a higher percentage than the 82 percent of fee-for-service patients who expressed satisfaction with their providers.

Objective measures

More objective efforts to determine whether HMOs have accomplished what they set out to do—that is, reduce costs while at the same time providing quality health care—have also been undertaken. Many of those studies have found that the quality of care in HMOs is better than or as good as care given in the fee-for-service setting and that HMOs are successfully holding down costs. A 1996 study by the research firm of KPMG Peat Marwick, for example, surveyed cities with high HMO membership levels. That study found that "costs were 11 percent lower, hospital stays 6 percent shorter, and death rates 5 percent lower than in cities where most care was provided under fee-for-service arrangements."[7]

The *American Journal of Public Health* has reported that managed care providers have a better record concerning the early detection of certain cancers. HMOs diagnose older women with breast cancer in the earliest stages—when the disease is most treatable—72 percent of the time, for example, compared to 66 percent in the fee-for-service setting.

Yet another study, this one published in the *Journal of the American Medical Association*, considered costs and outcomes of treatment for several chronic illnesses. The results were again favorable. HMO doctors used 40 percent fewer hospital days and 12 percent fewer drugs than fee-

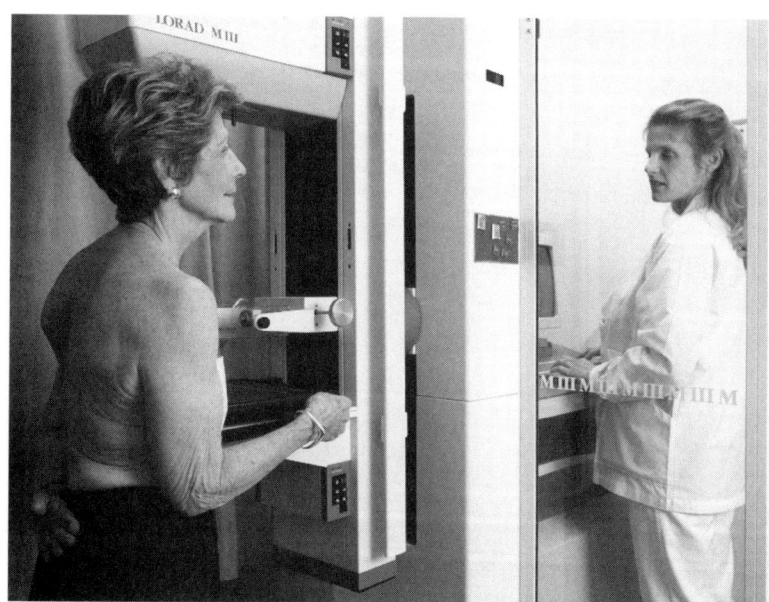

Some studies indicate that HMOs excel at detecting breast cancer while it is in an early stage of development.

for-service doctors and with equally good outcomes for their patients.

Studies such as these convince many experts that HMOs and other managed care providers are succeeding in their goals. Says David Nash, an HMO expert at Jefferson Medical College in Philadelphia, "Overwhelmingly, the published evidence supports the notion that quality of care in the managed care arena equals, if not surpasses, the care in the private, fee-for-service sector."[8]

Lost in the system

Though managed care appears to deliver the greatest amount of health care services to the greatest number of people, it often falls short of meeting individual needs. Because patients must use providers within the plan's network, and because doctors' schedules are often filled for weeks in advance, a patient may have to see a different doctor at each visit. Patients sometimes feel more like parts of the system than individuals with feelings and needs.

Managed care organizations have also been accused of placing cost considerations ahead of medical needs. Prescription drugs are one example. Managed care organizations have a reference guide called a formulary. It lists the names of the medications the organization will pay for when doctors prescribe them. Whenever a generic form of a drug is available, doctors must prescribe it rather than the brand-name product. To order the brand-name version, or a drug that is not in the formulary at all, doctors must write a statement justifying the need for such an exception. The managed care organization then decides whether the justification is valid. If the organization rejects the justification, the patient can still get the prescription, but he or she will have to pay most or all of its cost.

Though this approach saves the managed care company millions of dollars in pharmaceutical costs each year, it may increase the burdens on patients and doctors. Patients may be required to try a progression of drugs to prove that the ones on the formulary are ineffective before their doctors are permitted to prescribe a nonformulary drug. Doctors complain that administrators are making decisions that should be left to medical professionals. Doctors sometimes feel that the decision to exclude a drug from the formulary is based more on the drug's costs than on its potential benefits. "I never thought I would have to deal with trying to justify giving care to someone," says Mark Brooks. "Now we're told, no, the patient can't have that, as a seemingly arrogant decision made by someone who doesn't know the facts."[9]

The gatekeeper

This concern goes to the heart of complaints about managed care. Many physicians and patients alike see managed care as the gatekeeper for health care services. Instead of letting people through to needed services, critics claim that managed care focuses on keeping them out. In most managed care systems, a patient must see a primary care doctor first. The primary care doctor decides whether to treat the patient or refer him or her to a specialist. Some managed care organizations require doctors to obtain approval for a referral. A patient who sees a specialist without a referral, or a specialist who is not part of the managed care system's network, may have to pay the full costs for the visit and any treatment.

Horror stories abound in the media about patients who could not get the care they needed because their referrals were delayed or denied. The role of managed care and insurance company administrators—nonphysicians and often nonmedical staff—in making decisions about what care will be covered worries many physicians. Though administrators say they are only making coverage, not medical, decisions, whether a patient receives the test or treatment the doctor feels is necessary typically depends on whether it will be covered.

Battles between patients and their insurance companies sometimes erupt publicly, as was the case in 1999 when Washington state resident James Ellison fought his managed care company over coverage for treating his multiple sclerosis. The thirty-seven-year-old man had a particularly aggressive form of multiple sclerosis that was rapidly destroying his nervous system. Ellison's doctors said his only hope was a stem-cell transplant, a sophisticated procedure that his insurance company would not cover because it was experimental. Despite the support of state insurance commissioner Deborah Senn, Ellison lost his fight with his insurance company. In an unusual turn of events, an anonymous donor stepped forward to pay seventy-five thousand dollars of the one-hundred-thousand-dollar fee. Ellison had the procedure, which arrested his multiple sclerosis. He and his doctors remain optimistic about a long-term benefit.

Stories such as this have prompted changes in referral and approval procedures. Many managed care organizations have established detailed guidelines for physicians to follow in making testing and treatment recommendations. Doctors are allowed to order nonstandard tests and treatments when they believe that doing so is the best option for the patient, but the costs are charged to the doctor's department or practice group. When these costs exceed the money budgeted to pay for nonstandard care, the HMO can reduce the doctor's compensation to recover its losses. Managed care administrators say this gives doctors the flexibility to go outside the system when they feel it is necessary to do so. Critics say the approach still puts money before care by forcing doctors to consider the costs of their decisions rather than focusing on what is medically best for the patient.

Another approach that many managed care organizations have implemented puts controversial decisions, such as denying coverage for a new but largely untested cancer treatment, in the hands of review panels that include physician experts. Some states have established independent review panels that remove the decision making from the insurance company once a person appeals the company's determination.

Keeping managed care healthy

Many HMOs are attempting to resolve criticisms of their approach by making changes in the ways they operate. "We can be a catalyst and an organizer in what is presently a fragmented system," says Ruth Shuck, chief executive officer of the South Carolina–based HMO HealthFirst. "We can organize care and make it easier for people to receive services, and we can do it without getting between the doctor and the patient."[10]

Some managed care plans are experimenting with different models of service, such as allowing physicians to make referrals to the specialists of their choice even if those specialists are not in the HMO's network. The physicians must be willing to accept financial penalties for excessive costs, however, such as reduced compensation or "borrowing" against the next year's budget. Some managed care plans are even extending a similar option to patients by providing a higher level of coverage for services provided through the HMO and a limited level of coverage for services received outside the HMO.

Elected officials are keeping a close eye on the evolution of managed care, too. Many states have passed, or plan to introduce, laws defining the rights patients have in dealing with managed care systems. In September 1999 in California, for example, the governor signed a package of bills offering new rights, coverage, and protections to 23 million state residents who are covered by HMOs. According to a news report, the legislative package of twenty-one bills

An infectious disease doctor checks her records. Some managed care plans allow physicians to make referrals to specialists of their choice.

provides new ways for patients to challenge HMO decisions, including a guarantee of a second opinion, a new independent review system and the right to sue if they have been substantially harmed. . . . [It] requires health plans to cover severe mental illness, contraceptives, cancer screening, diabetes and phenylketonuria, or PKU, a rare genetic disease. . . . [It] establishes a new state agency to regulate health care plans. . . . [It] provides new protections for patient privacy.[11]

The U.S. Congress has also been struggling with issues related to managed care. Both the House of Representatives and the Senate introduced numerous bills in 1998 and 1999 in an attempt to give consumers greater legal rights in their health care decisions. Most of these efforts targeted managed care plans, attempting to limit and control their ability to override physician recommendations. While philosophical disagreements between Democrats and Republicans stalled passage of the bills, the intense debate spurred the managed care industry to make some changes itself. In late 1999, the nation's second-largest such company changed its policy to allow doctors to make final decisions, based solely on medical criteria, in disputed coverage situations.

One hope that analysts hold for the future of health care in America is that the key players—physicians, hospitals, and insurance companies—will work together to develop health care delivery systems that work smoothly and efficiently for the patients who use them. Many believe that managed care has the potential to be this collaboration.

2

Rationing Health Care

FEW AMERICANS, IF given the choice, would deny themselves or their loved ones access to lifesaving medical technology and care even if the cost is high and the chance for recovery is uncertain. The idea of limiting or rationing health care to hold down costs or to make health care available to more people has little appeal. A 1994 *Newsweek* poll confirmed this when it found that 78 percent of survey participants objected to limiting their choice of doctors and hospitals for the purpose of reducing costs and broadening access to health care. In addition, 60 percent of those polled rejected limits on their use of specialists and technology.

Despite strong objections to health care rationing, rationing has become a reality in some fields of medicine. One such field is organ transplants. Every year the number of people who require organ transplants far outstrips the supply of donor organs. There is much debate about who should receive donated organs, who should have priority, and how to make such decisions. The issues that surround the allocation of donated organs for transplants offer insight into concerns that may soon affect many fields of medicine.

Prioritizing limited resources

Organ transplants have become a standard treatment of last resort in America for patients whose own kidneys, livers, lungs, corneas, and hearts fail. Every year there are nearly sixty thousand people on waiting lists for replacement organs. Fewer than twenty thousand of them will receive the transplants they need.

The biggest reason why so few patients receive their needed transplants is due to the limited supply of donor organs. Organ donation is voluntary. Some organs—bone marrow, for example—come from a living donor. Most donor organs come from accident victims who have signed donor cards or have told close relatives of their desire to donate organs in case of accidental death. Fewer than 15 percent of Americans actually sign donor cards; even when an accident victim has signed a donor card, there is no guarantee that a person's organs will be used.

The criteria for organ donation is strict. To qualify, the donor must die in a hospital while on life-support systems. After death occurs, life-support systems keep oxygen-rich blood circulating through the organs and, in particular, the heart. When life-support systems keep the heart beating after death has occurred, the person is technically considered

Doctors prepare for kidney transplant surgery. Because of the shortage of organ donors, some patients never receive needed transplants.

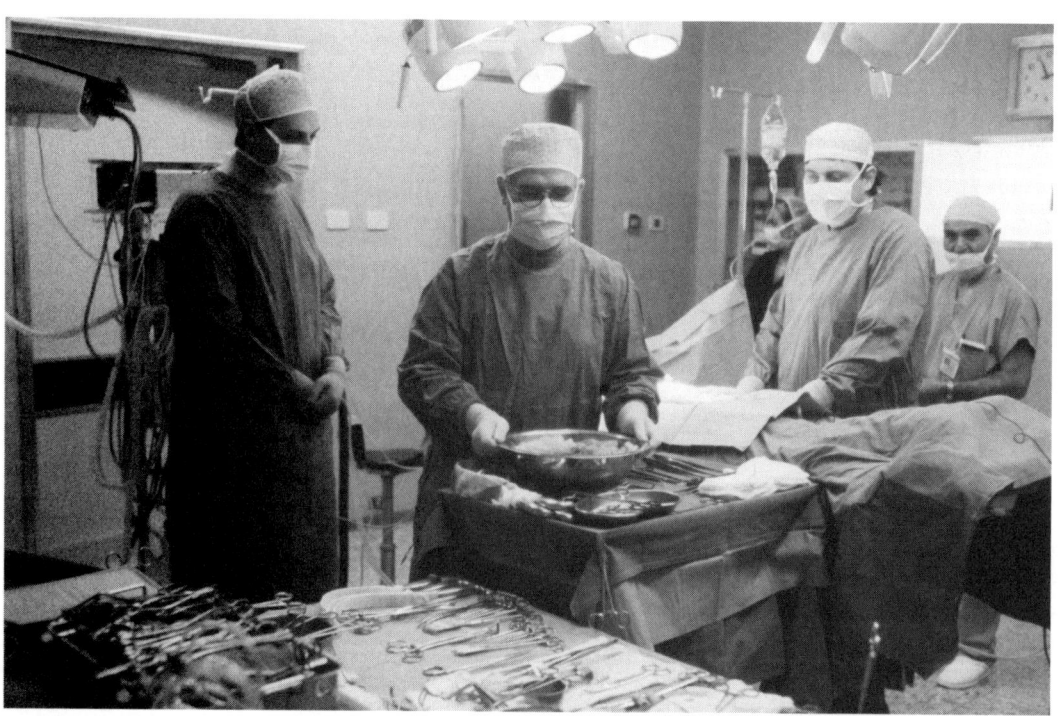

brain dead. The organs must be taken, or harvested, after brain death occurs but before life support is turned off. Even when a person has signed a donor card, the consent of a close relative is often required. Without that consent, healthy organs may not be harvested in time.

The current distribution system has long relied on voluntary cooperation among hospitals and doctors to maintain patient waiting lists and notification procedures. A not-for-profit organization called the United Networks for Organ Sharing (UNOS) oversees donor organ distribution. Doctors and hospitals follow the UNOS guidelines for harvesting and transplanting organs. These guidelines also establish the criteria for a patient's priority on the waiting list. Patients near death have the highest priority. UNOS maintains a computer database of all the waiting lists. There is a separate list for each type of organ transplant. When a donor organ becomes available, it goes to the sickest person on the waiting list who is closest to the donor location. The organ must also be a match for the patient; if the organ is incompatible with the patient's tissue type, the patient's body will reject it.

The average wait for a donor kidney, which is the most common organ needed for transplant, is sixteen months. Many of those on a transplant list will die before a donor organ becomes available. Others will stay on the waiting list, moving up in priority as they become sicker. While moving up in priority increases the chance of getting a donor organ, the chance of long-term success diminishes as the patient's condition worsens. This is a significant dilemma for experts struggling to maintain an equitable organ distribution system. Giving priority to the sickest patients often means bypassing the patients who have the best odds for surviving surgery and returning to productive lives. Yet passing over the sickest patients dooms them to certain death.

To the patient awaiting a new liver or heart, calculations about the odds of success may seem a cruel exercise. But the choice of who receives an organ and who does not has broad consequences given the limited organ supply and the high cost of organ transplant operations. A kidney transplant, for example, costs at least fifty thousand dollars. A heart transplant costs ten times that amount. A failed transplant means the loss of a viable organ and a huge waste of money. It may also mean the death of two patients: the one who received the transplant and the one who did not.

The dilemmas of limited supply

The limited supply of donor organs and the costs of transplants have created a dilemma over how to allocate available organs. Some experts believe that this system, despite its flaws, is the most equitable. They say one reason it works so well is that local hospitals and doctors know their efforts to harvest donor organs will benefit local people. This encourages them to seek permission from next of kin to harvest organs, which is often a difficult and emotional process. Donor organs have the greatest chance of functioning properly when they are transplanted immediately. Sending the organs to patients who are long distances away takes valuable time.

Others feel this system has been anything but equitable. The list of people needing organs is divided by regions of the country. When an organ becomes available, it goes to the most appropriate person within the region where the donor is at the time. Because so many organ donors are the unfortunate victims of car accidents, and because car accidents are more numerous in urban rather than rural locations, more donor organs become available in metropolitan areas. Some critics oppose this system because it shortchanges people who do not live in metropolitan areas. They believe that donor organs should be distributed to the person with the greatest medical need as long as the organ can be safely transported to that person before it expires. Because commercial jets can fly coast to coast in six hours, they suggest, this option is viable.

This view recently gained strength in the longrunning policy debate. New rules issued by the Department of Health and Human Services require UNOS to send organs to the sickest patients first, no matter where they live. The new rules were to take effect by January 2000. However, strong opposition to the change foreshadowed a delay and possible postponement.

A stickier issue is that of determining when and whether a patient should be placed on an organ transplant list. In many cases, the diseases that make organ transplants necessary are direct or indirect results of lifestyle choices and habits. Cigarette smoking, for example, is the leading cause of heart disease in America and is therefore a leading reason for many heart transplant operations. Many liver transplants in adults are necessary because years of alcohol abuse have destroyed the patient's liver. These factors have never been considered in determining whether a person qualifies for an organ transplant, though others such as age and the presence of multiple ailments often are considerations. Most people over age sixty do not qualify for heart transplants, for example, because they typically have other health problems that make them poor candidates for such stressful surgery. With donor hearts in such short supply, doctors must be sure that those who receive them have a reasonable chance for recovery. The increasing gap between needed and available donor organs may force doctors to consider a patient's lifestyle choices in deciding who gets an organ and who does not.

Alcohol abuse is a major contributor to liver damage.

Perceptions of preferential treatment

Several high-profile cases have brought these issues into the public spotlight, most notably the liver transplants of rock musician David Crosby and baseball great Mickey Mantle.

At age fifty-three, Crosby had a history of extensive drug abuse that had destroyed his liver. Without a transplant, he would die. "There was no question . . . that substance abuse did, in fact, contribute to the condition of David's liver,"[12] Eliot Mintz, the musician's publicist, told a California newspaper following Crosby's transplant surgery in 1994.

Some medical ethicists questioned whether someone like Crosby—whose condition resulted from lifestyle choices—deserved to receive one of the few livers available at the time. Public perception was that Crosby got his lifesaving transplant because of his fame, though his doctors and the hospital where his surgery was performed said Crosby's case followed the standard guidelines. Others argued that it was inequitable and inconsistent to punish an individual for making poor decisions. Doing so was counter to the physician's responsibility to treat patients without judgment. They noted that Crosby's lifestyle was common knowledge only because he was a celebrity. To deny him an organ on the basis of lifestyle while not holding others to the same standard would be unfair.

Similar issues surfaced a few months later when baseball legend Mickey Mantle received a liver transplant. Mantle had abused alcohol for decades and damaged his liver in the process. When he entered the hospital in June 1995, his only chance to leave alive was a transplant. The

Although the average wait for a new liver is one hundred days, baseball star Mickey Mantle received one in less than a month.

surgery was a success, but a few weeks later doctors announced that Mantle had liver cancer, which greatly reduced his chance for survival. Many in the organ transplant community felt that Mantle had received an organ that would not have gone to him had he not been a celebrity. Mantle's doctors, like Crosby's, insisted that their famous patient had not received special treatment. Mantle died two months after receiving a new liver. He was sixty-three.

Both Crosby and Mantle waited less than a month for new livers at a time when the average wait was just over one hundred days. This gave rise to the perception that they were able to "buy" priority on the waiting list because of their star status. However, Crosby was in Los Angeles and Mantle in Dallas—both locations where organ supply and medical expertise are abundant and average wait times are typically shorter than in more remote areas.

Making the choice to limit health care services

While the nationwide debate over organ distribution continues, one state is already establishing priorities and setting limits on organ transplants and many other medical procedures. Motivated by costs that far exceeded projections, the state of Oregon decided in 1987 to stop paying for organ transplants for Medicaid patients. Lawmakers felt the money the state spent to benefit relatively few people could better serve the overall population by extending basic health services to more people. The Oregon legislature, working in coalition with providers, insurers, and citizens, embarked on a six-year journey that would result in the nation's first formalized plan for rationing health care services.

The plan the Oregon coalition developed, which became known as the Oregon Health Plan (OHP), focused on providing the most health care services to the greatest number of people to produce the most positive health outcomes. Through a series of community and professional forums, the coalition gathered data and information from residents and health care providers about what the plan should and should not cover. What emerged was a prioritized list of

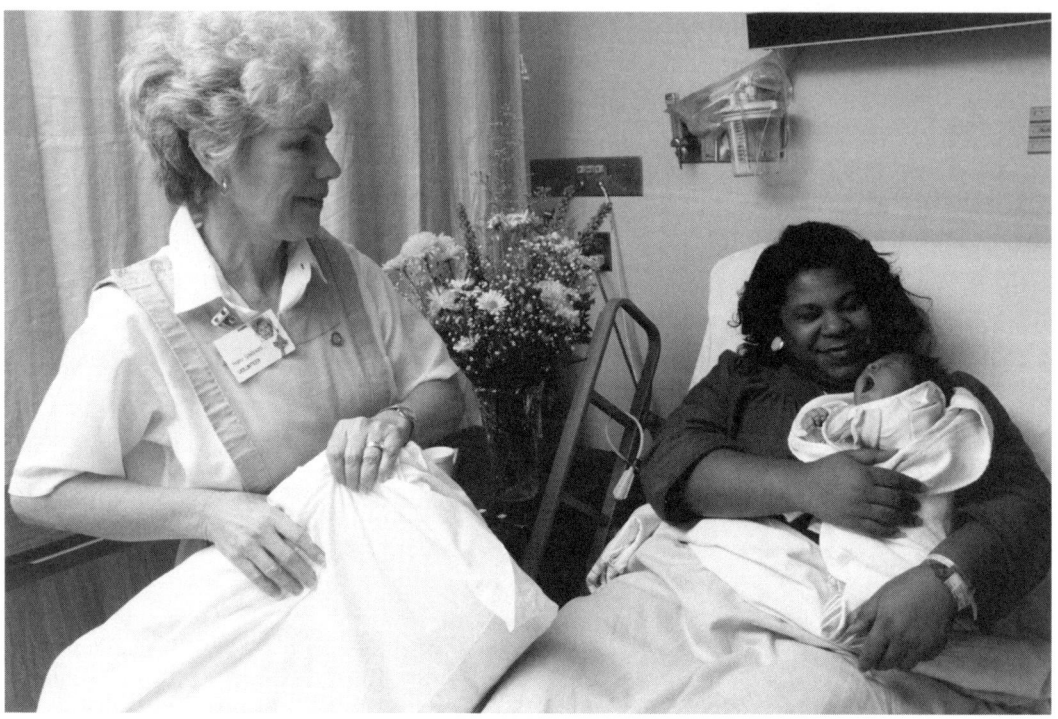

Maternity care is among the services covered by the Oregon Health Plan.

nearly eight hundred health care services. High on the list were basic health and preventive care services such as doctor visits and hospital services for illness, maternity care, and routine medical and dental checkups. Low on the list were cosmetic surgery, pain clinics, and weight-loss programs. Expensive, high-tech procedures such as bone marrow transplants are ranked according to their ability to prevent death, an emphasis that considers both short- and long-term success.

The first version of the OHP was implemented in 1994. Every two years, the Oregon legislature reviews the prioritized list and establishes the OHP budget. OHP administrators then determine who qualifies for OHP coverage. Generally, these are Oregon residents who have annual incomes near or below the federal poverty level, though eligibility can vary with funding. The OHP pays for their health care services according to the prioritized list. Not all needed services are covered at the same level, and covered services may vary with budget cycles as the legislature allocates more or less funding. The result, says physician Andrew Glass, who served on the state's Health Services Commission, is a program that provides health care services for the poor by identifying "*what* gets treated, not *who* gets treated."[13] This approach attempts to shift decision making away from emotional or financial considerations and toward proven medical techniques and care options that offer clear benefit for the greatest number of people.

Critics, however, contend that the opposite has occurred. The original intention in Oregon was to extend basic health services to all Oregon residents, but this has not happened. Instead, only the state's poorest residents, those who rely on government-funded Medicaid, are subject to health care rationing. So what might have started as an effort to create an egalitarian system, critics say, is actually now based entirely on income level. Writer and commentator Nat Hentoff addressed these concerns in a 1992 article for the *Village Voice* newspaper:

Proponents of the Oregon Health Plan observe that more people in Oregon now have access to services such as dental care.

> Will government—federal, state, and local—be allowed to use a utilitarian measure—the greatest good for the greatest number—to decide who gets care and who doesn't? . . . Under this [Oregon] plan . . . the poor are pitted against each other while the bureaucrats decide which of the poor shall survive.[14]

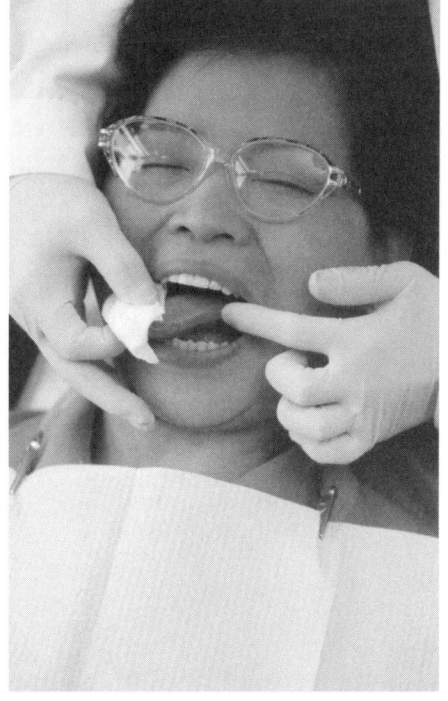

Advocates of the OHP note that more people in the state of Oregon now have access to routine, basic health care services, including mental health and dental care, than did under the previous traditional Medicaid plan. Such accessibility encourages people to seek care in the early stages of illness or injury, when treatment is relatively low cost. One result has been a decrease in Medicaid payments for expensive emergency room care. Another has been an increase in the number of people who have a regular primary care provider. Nearly two hundred thousand Oregon residents who previously had no health insurance became eligible for the OHP in its first four years of existence.

The OHP does precisely what analysts say a fair rationing program must do—it removes the emphasis from the individual and places it on the resource. If such a program were expanded nationwide, health care reform advocates say, more Americans would have access to health care services than are now possible.

Most experts agree that some level of health care rationing is inevitable. The allocation system currently in place for organ transplants and the debate surrounding the Oregon Health Plan illustrate the challenges that the health care industry faces in trying to develop methods that are both efficient and fair. Continuing advances in medical technology will mean great improvements in health care for many people. These advances will also mean an increased need on the part of doctors and other health care providers to make decisions about which patients should receive costly and sophisticated tests and treatments, perhaps based on different criteria than those used in the past. Notes health care writer Willard Gaylin, "When that which we are rationing is life itself, the decisions as to how, what, and when must be made by a consensus. . . . Although the idea of explicit rationing created a furor at first, most Oregonians came to accept it. Most other Americans will have to do the same."[15]

3

Keeping Communities Healthy

MAINTAINING PUBLIC HEALTH in a nation of nearly 275 million people is no simple task. It takes a coordinated effort among various entities—doctors, government agencies, public health programs, schools, and individuals. These efforts have paid off in many ways.

Today, diseases that annually claim thousands of lives around the world are rarely fatal in America. Pertussis, also known as whooping cough, was once the leading cause of death in children in the United States, killing twelve thousand children each year. Today fewer than one thousand cases a year are reported in America, and most of these are in adults who survive the disease without complications. Measles, listed as one of the top six causes of death in children worldwide, is now also rare in the United States. Fewer than three hundred cases of measles were reported nationwide in 1995.

The near elimination of many fatal diseases in this country can be attributed to a high immunization rate and the widespread use of antibiotics. Immunization, in particular, has greatly reduced the incidence of childhood diseases. More than 80 percent of American children routinely receive immunizations. That number contrasts with a 20-percent immunization rate worldwide.

Chronic hunger and malnutrition, which every year lead to millions of deaths and illnesses around the world, still exist in this nation, too, but on a vastly smaller scale than

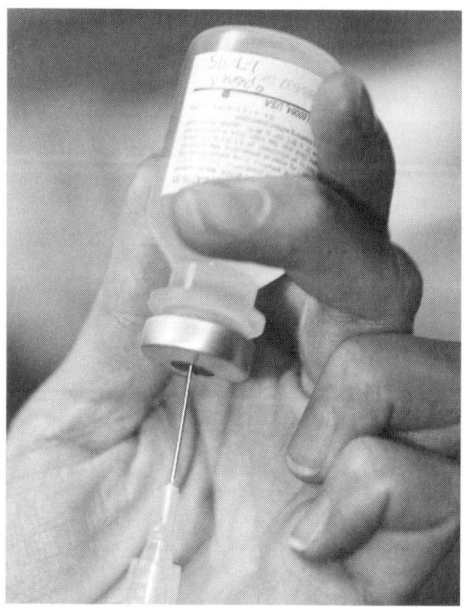

Immunizations are largely responsible for the near elimination of fatal diseases in the United States.

they occur elsewhere. Malnutrition afflicts 200 million children worldwide; half of them live in Asia. Malnutrition is a growing problem in sub-Saharan Africa, afflicting nearly a third of the children who live there. Though improving as the result of concentrated efforts by UNICEF, the United Nations, and other organizations, malnutrition and hunger remain a problem in Latin America and the Caribbean. Overall, malnutrition kills about 9 million people annually; about 6 million of those who die from starvation are children. Those who do not die, adults and children alike, often suffer from diseases related to malnutrition. Malnutrition also lowers resistance to disease. This makes those who are chronically hungry more susceptible to infections such as pneumonia, which is now the leading cause of death due to infection among children worldwide. A high living standard as well as government programs such as food stamps and private ventures such as food banks have helped reduce these problems in the United States.

Two important indicators of health

Despite impressive gains in eliminating many diseases and feeding the nation's population, the United States ranks low in two important areas: life expectancy and infant mortality. Life expectancy—how long a person can expect to live—and infant mortality—how many infants die before their first birthdays—are two of the most important indicators of a nation's overall health. Because an infant's survival and life expectancy depend on a variety of health, nutrition, and social factors, these rates present a fairly comprehensive snapshot of a community's general state of wellness. In each case, the United States ranks low among the world's developed nations. The average life expectancy in the United States of just over seventy-five years ranks seventeenth, and the nation's infant mortality rate of 7.1 (just over seven deaths for every one thousand births) ranks twenty-fifth among developed countries.

Experts suggest a number of explanations for America's poor showing in these two health indicators. One of the most often cited explanations is lifestyle. Overeating, lack of exercise, cigarette smoking, alcohol abuse, sexual promiscuity, and a high rate of teen pregnancy are among the primary causes of health problems in America today. These behaviors contribute to seven of the ten leading causes of death in the United States: heart disease, lung disease, cancer, diabetes, AIDS, stroke, and liver disease.

The number-one cause of death in America today, for example, is heart disease. Every day twenty-six hundred Americans die from heart disease. Researchers believe as many as 80 percent of those deaths could have been prevented through lifestyle changes. Cigarette smoking, poor diet, and lack of exercise are the main causes of heart disease. By lowering the level of fat in the diet, exercising at least thirty minutes a day four times a week, and not smoking, experts say, heart disease could be greatly reduced. However, fewer than 40 percent of Americans engage in any kind of regular exercise. More than half of the nation's population is overweight. And cigarette smoking, especially among young people, is on the rise. Convincing

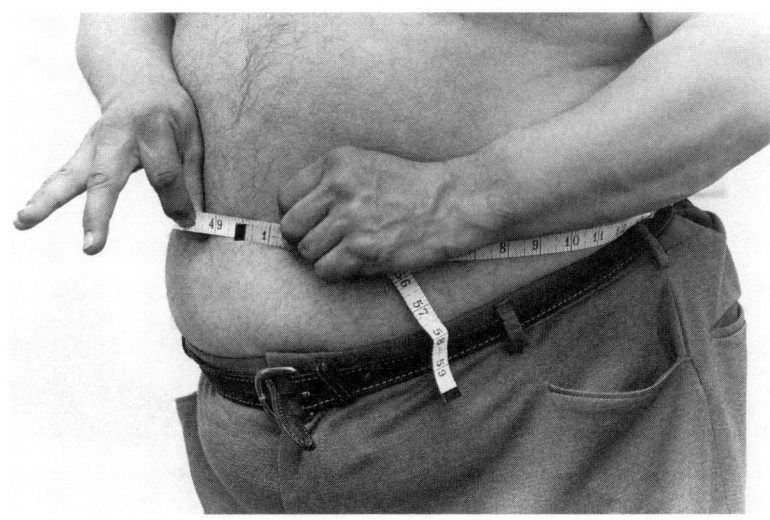

Obesity is one of the primary causes of health problems in America.

Americans to change their behavior and lifestyle represents a significant challenge to those charged with maintaining public health.

Unhealthy choices

In the United States, poor diet usually results from poor choices rather than from the absence of healthful foods. For example, a recent study showed that half of California residents who eat out choose fast food over more nutritious options. Among those surveyed, a third had eaten a high-fat, high-sugar item such as cake or a doughnut and one in five had eaten fried items on the day they answered the survey questions.

"The study paints a bleak picture for public health," says California public health official James W. Stratton. "We live in the richest agricultural state in the world, yet we're passing up healthy foods like fruits, vegetables, and low fat milk for foods high in fat and added sugar. These eating habits will cause more illness, premature deaths, and increased healthcare costs."[16]

Substituting high-fat food for more nutritious options can result in diabetes or obesity.

The link between poor eating habits and poor health is well known. Diabetes and obesity are just two of the possible conditions that may result from poor nutrition, and obesity is becoming a major health concern. Obesity is known to increase the risk for a number of health problems, including early coronary artery disease, Type 2 diabetes, and high blood pressure. It may also lead to early death. A 1999 article in the *New England Journal of Medicine* reports the findings of a fourteen-year study involving more than a million Americans that suggests that obesity doubles an individual's likelihood of dying from any cause. About a third of Americans—60 million people—are considered obese, meaning they weigh more than 20 percent over the recommended weight for their height.

The importance of exercise

Diet is only one half of a healthy lifestyle, however. Exercise is the other half. Health experts recommend a minimum of thirty minutes of moderate activity, such as walking, four days a week to maintain good health and prevent lifestyle-related medical problems. Less than half of Americans get this much exercise, and as many as 20 percent get almost no physical activity at all. Lack of exercise among children is a particular concern. Regular exercise is important for proper growth of bones and muscles. Young people who do not exercise risk developing health problems such as obesity, diabetes, and heart disease at an early age. Doctors today say they are already seeing more young patients with conditions that usually affect people over age sixty.

Some experts believe that exercise is even more important than diet in maintaining health. Chemicals released by the body during exercise affect the functions of cells

A healthy lifestyle can be attained through healthy diet and regular exercise.

throughout the body, which can alter everything from blood pressure to mood. Regular exercise appears to affect the way the body uses and stores fat, too, which has important implications for those at risk for developing heart disease. Even mild exercise benefits health problems such as arthritis and back pain.

Smoking

Efforts to eat nutritiously and exercise regularly can be in vain if a person also smokes cigarettes. Few lifestyle habits affect health more negatively than cigarette smoking. Nearly five hundred thousand Americans die each year from smoking-related diseases. Cigarette smoking is the leading cause of heart disease, lung cancer and other lung diseases, and mouth and throat cancer.

Cigarette smoking carries risks for more than the smoker. A pregnant woman who smokes risks the health and proper development of her fetus. Studies show that smoking interferes with the flow of oxygen to the fetus, which may affect brain development and birth weight. It can also lead to asthma or even to death. Researchers also believe that people who live and work around smokers can suffer health effects similar to those experienced by smokers. Studies show, for example, that young children who live in homes where they are continually exposed to cigarette smoke are more likely to suffer from ear infections and upper respiratory problems.

Despite an abundance of information about the harm of smoking and long-running public health campaigns aimed at reducing smoking, it is still a common habit. The percentage of adult Americans who smoke remains fixed at about 25 percent. The population of young people who smoke, for many years on the decline, began to climb in the 1990s, and this raises a great deal of concern among health care professionals. A 1997 University of Michigan study found that 37 percent of high-school seniors smoke cigarettes, the highest rate in nineteen years. Other studies suggest that nearly 4.5 million young people between the ages of twelve and seventeen smoke. Their health outlook is grim: If they continue smoking, half of them will die as a

direct result, and they will die at younger ages than their nonsmoking peers.

Smoking at a young age can result in long-term health problems and early death.

The health problems caused by smoking generally do not show up until after decades of cigarette use. This makes it difficult to convince people, especially young people, of the health dangers posed by cigarette smoking. It is easy for smokers early into the habit to convince themselves that they can quit whenever they wish and that they will not have health problems. The odds are not in their favor, however. According to the U.S. surgeon general, 90 percent of adults who smoke started smoking before age eighteen. A lifetime of smoking inevitably ends in a smoking-related disease. Smokers who quit before serious health problems set in have a good chance of reducing their risk of having one of these diseases.

Teen pregnancy

Young people often have difficulty seeing the long-term consequences of their actions—and not just where smoking is concerned. Thoughts of possible long-term consequences are not usually foremost in the minds of teenagers who engage in sexual activity. Nearly a million teenage girls became pregnant in 1998. Half of those girls gave birth; the other half had abortions. Though the American teen pregnancy rate dropped significantly during the 1990s, the United States leads developed countries in teen pregnancies. The United States has nearly twice as many teen pregnancies as England, for example, and eight times more than Japan.

Teen pregnancy is a public health issue for both teens and their babies. Younger teens, though they are biologically able to become pregnant, do not have fully developed bodies. Their bones are still growing, for instance, and require adequate amounts of calcium and other minerals. A growing fetus draws large amounts of minerals and vitamins from the mother's body, enough to deplete the supply even of a fully mature woman. Proper prenatal care uses vitamin and mineral supplements to offset this loss, keeping both mother and baby healthy.

Many teens do not receive proper prenatal care, however. Some are afraid to tell their parents that they are pregnant and do not know how to get care on their own. Others do not know that they are pregnant until the pregnancy is quite advanced, or they may convince themselves that they are not pregnant. Teens are often self-conscious about body image. Even a teen mother who is seeing a doctor may eat less than she should to avoid gaining weight.

The mother's behavior affects the baby's health as well as her own. Though the growing fetus will take as much nutrition from the mother as it can, it cannot take what is not there. An undernourished mother will most likely have an undernourished infant, who is at high risk for being born at low birth weight (weighing less than five and a half pounds). Low-birth-weight infants, especially those born prematurely, can have serious health problems, including lung and brain damage.

Regular health care during pregnancy helps assure adequate nutrition, which is a critical factor in the fetus's development. Prenatal care also detects many health problems in the mother that can affect the baby, such as the presence of sexually transmitted diseases. Infants born to women who receive little or no prenatal care are four times more likely to die before their first birthdays than are the babies of women who begin receiving regular care early in pregnancy.

Sexually transmitted diseases

Sexual activity among young people and nonmonogomous adults poses additional challenges for public health workers. Despite numerous prevention and treatment options, sexually transmitted diseases, also called STDs, remain a significant health problem in the United States today. There are nearly seventy thousand cases of sexually

Women weigh in at a prenatal care clinic. Pregnant teenagers often suffer from lack of prenatal care.

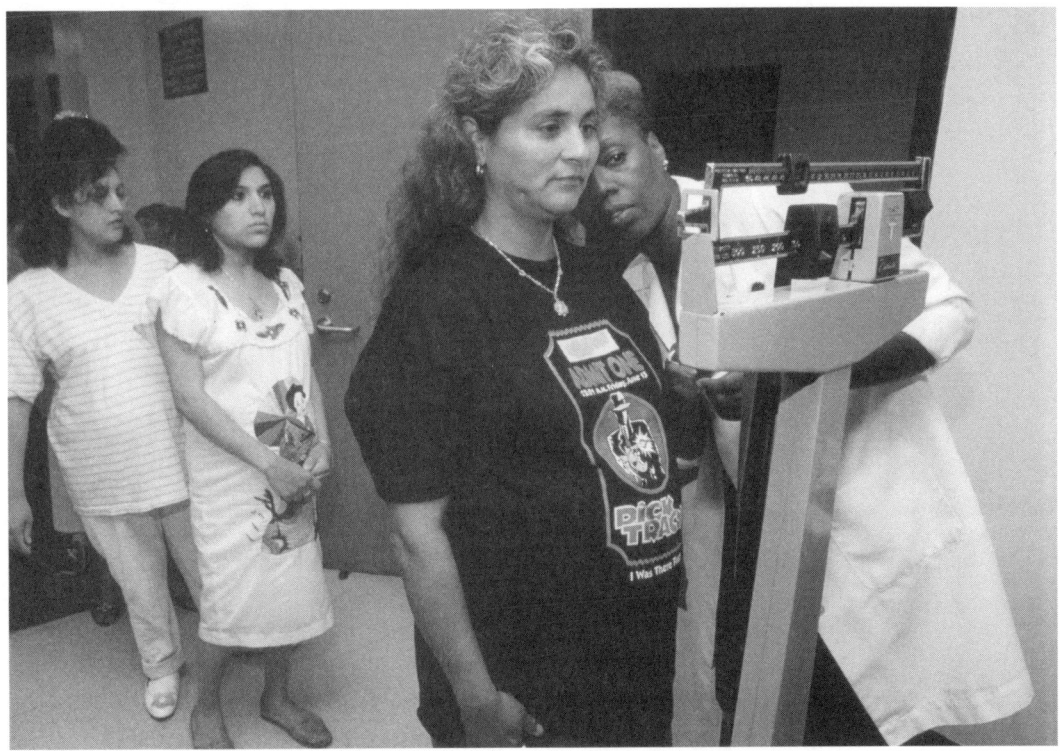

transmitted diseases in the United States each year. The risk of contracting the most common of these diseases—chlamydia, gonorrhea, and syphilis—can be greatly reduced through the use of a condom during sexual intercourse. All three are easily treated with antibiotics.

Unfortunately, these diseases often show no symptoms. Thus, up to 80 percent of women and 30 percent of men are unaware of their infections. Left untreated, sexually transmitted diseases can leave women and men infertile; some, such as syphilis, can damage tissues and organs, including the heart and brain. Newborn infants can also suffer the effects of untreated sexually transmitted disease. Doctors routinely place antibiotic drops in the eyes of infants at birth to safeguard against eye infections that can result from untreated gonorrhea in the mother. Such infections can cause permanent eye damage and blindness.

Public health campaigns—stressing condom use and regular testing for those who engage in risky sexual behavior—have had some effect on the incidence of these diseases. In 1999, for example, public health officials recorded just under four thousand new cases of syphilis, the lowest number of new cases since record keeping for STDs began in 1941.

Health workers hope for similar success in their campaign to teach people about AIDS. There is currently no cure for AIDS, which is a fatal sexually transmitted disease that can also be spread through shared needles. While new drugs and drug combinations can keep people alive longer once they have been infected by HIV, the virus that causes AIDS, onset of the disease leads to death.

AIDS education efforts have centered on methods of prevention, including abstinence, condom use, monogomous relationships, and avoiding needle-sharing between users of intravenous drugs. For many, these efforts have come too late. By the mid-1990s, more than three hundred thousand Americans had died of AIDS. Although the death rate began dropping in 1988 after the introduction of powerful new drugs, the federal Centers for Disease Control (CDC) estimates that as many as a million others are living

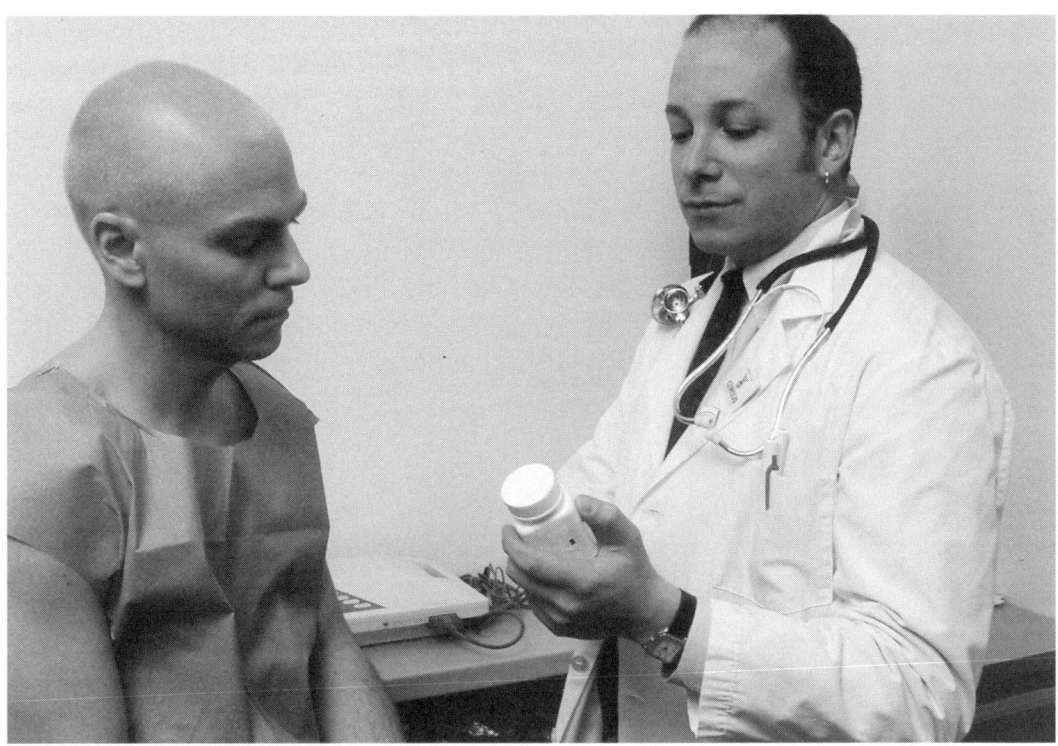

with HIV (and often don't know it), and forty thousand of them will develop AIDS each year.

A doctor treats an AIDS patient. There is no known cure for the deadly AIDS infection.

Keeping people healthy

Lifestyle will remain a significant challenge for future public health efforts. The U.S. Department of Health and Human Services, through its Office of Disease Prevention and Health Promotion, has developed an ambitious health initiative, Healthy People 2000 (and its successor, Healthy People 2010), that establishes health objectives and the steps necessary to meet them. This framework for national prevention and wellness efforts developed in 1990 has three overriding goals: "1. Increase the years of healthy life for Americans; 2. Reduce health disparities among Americans; and 3. Achieve access to preventive services for all Americans."[17]

Periodic reviews monitor and report progress toward these goals in each of twenty-two priority areas. More than

650 agencies and organizations throughout the country support Healthy People 2000, which met or exceeded 15 percent of its objectives and showed progress in nearly half of the others in 1999. This set the stage for Healthy People 2010, a continuation of the nation's health improvement goals that refines and adjusts health objectives and their measures. Many of these goals emphasize the lifestyle factors that affect health and disease. Most health experts agree that an old adage is particularly relevant: An ounce of prevention is worth a pound of cure.

4

The Doctor Shortage in Rural America

THE UNITED STATES has more doctors now than ever before. There were nearly seven hundred thousand doctors in active practice in 1999, twice as many as in 1970 and ten times more than in 1940. Yet for 50 million Americans, a trip to the doctor requires a long-distance commute. These Americans live in rural areas where the nearest medical services might be fifty or one hundred miles away. Two-thirds of the nation's roughly three thousand counties do not have the doctors they need. Federal guidelines call for there to be a minimum of one doctor for every three-thousand five-hundred people. In 1998 America's rural communities fell short of this standard by nearly five thousand doctors.

In 1996, for example, five Colorado counties had no primary care physicians and many of the state's other counties failed to reach the federal minimum standard. This has raised concern about the quality of medical services in rural areas. "We've got 63 counties in this state—and parts of 57 have shortages based on federal guidelines," Lindy Nelson, director of the state's Rural and Primary Health Policy and Planning office, said in 1996. "It's compromising the quality of health care for our rural residents."[18]

The problem of too few doctors in rural communities is not new. When Dean Branson set up his practice in south-central Colorado in the late 1980s, he was the only full-time physician for more than 3,000 square miles. But

49

experts contend that the doctor shortage in the nation's rural areas is not getting better. Archer County, Texas, a community of eight thousand people spread across 950 square miles, is just one of the 150 U.S. counties that lacked a single doctor in 1998.

In terms of sheer numbers, there should be no shortage of doctors anywhere in the United States. America's 125 medical schools produce an abundance of new doctors, graduating 17,000 each year. At this rate, several studies suggest, there could be 165,000 more doctors than positions available for them by the year 2005. Some specialty areas are already experiencing a glut. Seven percent of doctors seeking jobs in specialties such as cardiology and internal medicine search six months or longer before finding a position. Yet family practice positions in hundreds of rural communities may go unfilled for years. A report from the Commission on Family Medicine, which surveyed health care needs in Colorado, concludes that "projections

Medical students study microbiology. Because most medical students work to become proficient in a specialty, there is a shortage of general practice doctors.

show continuing shortages in rural and frontier counties in 2005 and 2015, despite the fact that the state as a whole is projected to have a sufficient [doctor] supply."[19]

The specialist imbalance

If there are so many doctors, why is a trip to the doctor's office a major commute for 50 million Americans? One reason is a shift in the number of generalists and specialists. This shift has left some parts of the country with too many doctors and others with too few. The trend in medical education in recent years has been an increase in the number of doctors entering specialty fields and a decrease in the number of those studying general or family practice medicine. In 1996 more than two-thirds of the nation's doctors were specialists. By contrast, in 1961 more than half of American doctors were in general practice.

This shift has hit rural communities particularly hard. Specialists serve small segments of large populations. Though small communities have the same medical needs as large cities, too few people live in them to support the full complement of medical professionals found in big cities—general practitioners, pediatricians, cardiologists, radiologists, anesthesiologists, orthopedists, gynecologists, obstetricians, and others. The best that many small communities can hope for is to attract a general practitioner who can do everything from set broken bones to deliver babies. That's what they are least likely to find, however.

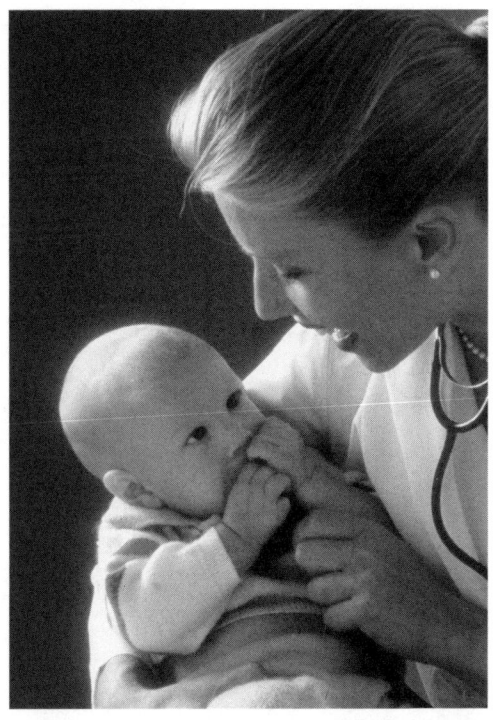

Many small towns lack specialists such as pediatricians.

The main reason for the oversupply of specialists and undersupply of generalists is financial. The average annual salary for a doctor in general practice is $135,000. A specialist can earn three to five times that amount. Many new doctors enter their careers with large school loans to pay off from the ten or more years of education they have completed to become doctors. Typically, rural medicine positions pay even less than the average salary, increasing the challenge for small communities to attract and keep qualified doctors.

Some experts believe it is the design of medical school programs that most significantly contributes to the supply imbalance between generalists and specialists. In the absence of specialists, doctors in rural areas must have a broad range of expertise to meet the diverse medical needs of their patients. They must be able to diagnose and treat everything from childhood diseases to conditions of aging such as heart disease. Few medical schools emphasize training in general practice, however. Most prepare graduates for further training in a specialty rather than for stepping into the role of the only doctor for hundreds of miles. "American medical education is the best in the world," says William Reynolds, president of the American College of Physicians. "But it's producing more physicians than we need, not always the kind of physicians most needed, and not always where they're needed."[20]

Encouraging doctors to go rural

To encourage new doctors to enter primary care practice in rural communities, a number of medical schools have established training programs in rural medicine. These programs put student doctors in rural communities, where they can get a feel for both the practice of rural medicine and the rural lifestyle. The first of these programs was the University of Minnesota's Rural Physician Associate Program, established in 1971. More than nine hundred of the university's medical students had completed the program by 1998. Of those who completed their education and established practice in the state of Minnesota, 64 percent returned to rural communities.

The Rural Physician Associate Program is considered a model for other rural medicine programs. It places student doctors in a rural setting for nine months, giving participants a fuller picture of small-town medical practice than they might get elsewhere. "For example, in a medical center, you seldom follow a natural pregnancy from start to finish," says Dr. Walter M. Swentko, who directs the program. "You see the patient at labor and delivery, and that's it. Further, you see the most difficult, complicated problems, not the ordinary. You learn that pregnancy is an abnormal complication of life, not a normal part of family living. You miss that this is a very normal experience we as doctors are invited to participate in."[21]

With such a long rotation, student doctors in the Rural Physician Associate Program also experience a bigger slice of community life. They have an opportunity to know their patients outside the clinic, which gives them a broader understanding of the lifestyle factors that contribute to health and disease. "In the rural setting, physicians bump into their patients in the grocery store, at church, on the softball field," Swentko says. "They get to know their patients as people, which doesn't often happen in large medical centers. And patients begin to see physicians as a way to make changes to improve health."[22]

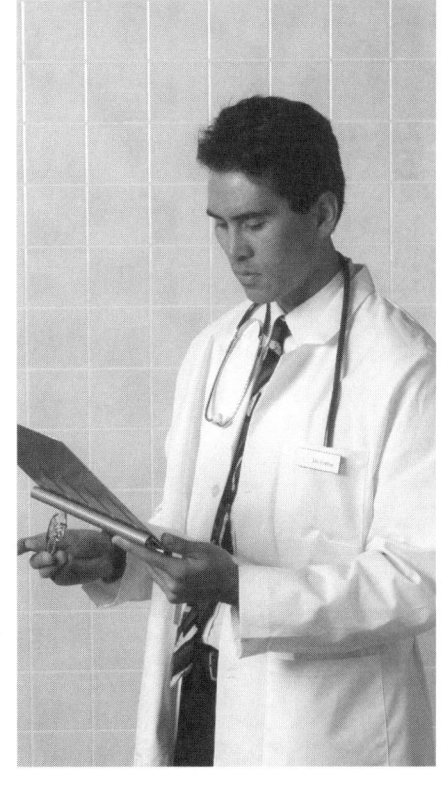

Some medical schools have established programs to lure doctors to rural communities.

The Thomas Jefferson University's Jefferson Medical College in Pennsylvania started its Physician Shortage Area Program in 1978 and has also seen a dramatic increase in new doctors entering rural medicine practice. Though the program's graduates represent just 1 percent of the new doctors that the state's seven medical schools produce each year, they account for 21 percent of the family physicians who practice in rural communities. The Jefferson program targets medical students who grew up in rural areas. These student doctors are already familiar with the characteristics of small communities, and many of them wish to return to their home communities as physicians. The Physician Shortage Area Program gives these students a head start on their goals by shaping their medical education from early in the process.

Programs to lure doctors to underserved areas typically offer financial incentives, usually in the form of scholarships or assistance in repaying school loans. Although these programs get doctors into rural communities for the short term, they have mixed success in getting doctors to stay once they complete their commitments. One such program is the federal government's National Health Service Corps. Started in 1970, the program offers scholarships to medical students and loan repayment packages to doctors who agree to practice up to three years in an area facing a doctor shortage. While the rural communities that benefit from the National Health Service Corps hope their temporary doctors will become permanent residents, studies suggest that this is not often the case. A 1993 study reported in the *Journal of the American Medical Association* found that only one in ten of these doctors remained in their rural community after fulfilling their commitments. This compared to four in ten who stayed after arriving in rural communities in other ways.

One explanation for this difficulty is motivation. Most doctors accept a National Health Services Corps assistance package to pay for their education, not because they want to work in underserved areas. Their service is an obligation in lieu of loan payments. Thus, they may have no genuine interest in rural medicine. Likewise, they may end up assigned to rural communities that are not good matches for their interests and expertise. A doctor with an interest in inner-city health care for children, for example, might end up in a sparsely populated community of mostly older adults in North Dakota.

Searching the world for qualified doctors

In an effort to find qualified doctors, many rural communities are turning for help to professional search companies. These firms advertise and network internationally, and they are often able to locate foreign doctors who want to live and practice in the United States. About fifteen hundred doctors from other countries obtain visas to come to America. Another twenty thousand international medical graduates enter American residency programs for further training, about 75 percent of whom stay to establish prac-

Getting to an emergency room quickly can increase an accident victim's chances of survival.

tices. These doctors are often willing to accept the offers small communities can make.

Although some critics complain that foreign doctors are taking positions away from American physicians, supporters are quick to point out that the communities that hire foreign doctors have often been searching for a doctor for years without success. Hiring foreign doctors, who are just as well trained as their American counterparts and must meet the licensing requirements of the state in which they practice, simply fills a void, supporters of the practice say. As one foreign doctor notes, "The place I am coming to is a rural community, an underserved community. So if I am occupying this [position], it's not that I'm taking anybody's chance."[23]

Leonardtown, Maryland, is one rural town that has literally built a medical community of foreign doctors over the years. Long drives for emergency care appealed much less to town officials and residents than the idea of hiring foreign doctors. Studies show that delays in emergency care often increase the chance of death from injuries sustained in an accident. The need to travel out of the county for emergency care was "almost like a death warrant"[24] for accident victims, says a local health officer.

Bringing the city to the country: telemedicine

Recruitment of foreign doctors is only one solution to the rural doctor shortage. Technology is another solution. Thanks to advances in telecommunications and computers, a doctor in even the most remote location can link to specialists and knowledge virtually anywhere in the world. Doctors in rural areas can send photos, X rays, and other patient information to specialists who can assist with diagnosis and treatment of any number of conditions.

For communities too small to support even a general doctor, telemedicine can also provide a connection to health care services. No longer does a specialist need to travel from, or a patient travel to, a distant medical center. In a trial program in the tiny town of Austin, Nevada, a registered nurse staffs a small clinic. Located 170 miles from the nearest hospital, this former silver mining community that was once the state's second-largest city now has fewer than one thousand residents. The health clinic has a computer, videoconferencing equipment, and basic medical supplies. The nurse examines patients who come to the clinic and handles many routine health care needs. When a patient's situation requires a doctor's attention, the nurse can use the computer to connect with a physician in Reno or Elko. The doctor and the patient can see and talk with each other using the computer's two-way video camera. The doctor can often make a diagnosis and prescribe appropriate treatment.

Telemedicine has been slow to gain widespread use, partly because it is expensive. A basic telemedicine station costs around forty thousand dollars to set up—and there must be a similar station at another location for the communication to take place. A survey conducted by the American Medical Association in 1996 showed that of the more than 2,400 rural hospitals across the country, only 350 used telemedicine. Another 200 or so facilities other than hospitals, such as clinics and nursing homes, used telemedicine also. "For decades, telemedicine has been touted as an essential element in the resurrection of rural medicine," according to a 1996 article in the *Journal of the*

American Medical Association. "Those expectations remain largely unrealized."[25]

Getting creative

While sophisticated technology helps some small communities overcome the doctor shortage, other communities have gotten creative in finding ways to attract doctors. They may provide a doctor's family with rent-free housing or arrange for special services such as childcare. Others focus on grooming their own doctors by targeting promising high school students and encouraging them to enter medicine.

Through teleconferencing, doctors are able to make a diagnosis and prescribe treatment for patients in rural areas without seeing them in person.

They may offer low interest loans and other assistance in exchange for a commitment to return to the community to practice medicine.

Though efforts such as these are successful in some areas with a doctor shortage, many more remain desperate for doctors. Colorado, for example, needs a new doctor every day for a year to reach the minimum number of doctors it should have for its population. More than 80 percent of the state's residents live in ten urban counties. The rest of the population is spread out over fifty-three counties, some of which have fewer than six people per square mile. Analysts predict that the shortage of doctors in Colorado's rural areas will worsen over the next ten to fifteen years, even though the state as a whole will have more than enough doctors. Many other states face similar challenges. "There have been lots and lots of programs in many states," says Lindy Nelson. "No one has come up with the magic solution yet about how this is going to work, how we're going to get more doctors in rural areas. Clearly what we've done is not enough."[26]

5

Caring for an Aging Population

AMERICANS ARE LIVING longer with each generation. According to the U.S. Census Bureau, half of this country's population was under age twenty in 1860. Few could expect to live to age sixty-five. In 1960, 6 out of every 100 Americans were age sixty-five or older. Just thirty-five years later, that figure had more than doubled, with 33.2 million Americans—more than 12 percent—over age sixty-five. Analysts project that by 2030, the number of Americans over age sixty-five will again double to 65 million—nearly 1 in 4.

The aging of America

Advances in medical technology and better living conditions share most of the credit for such dramatic increases. However, the rise in the number of Americans over age sixty-five is also the result of a dramatic increase in births between 1946 and 1964. During that period, 77 million babies were born in the United States—a 70 percent increase over the previous twenty years. This generation is often called the baby boom generation. Baby boomers will begin turning sixty-five in 2011, which will gradually raise the average age of Americans.

Some experts predict that this aging of America will have serious consequences for the health care system. The likelihood of serious medical conditions such as cancer and heart disease increases with age, which means that

*Senior citizens are
more likely than
younger people are to
suffer from serious
medical conditions.*

older people tend to use more health care services. Some
analysts worry that the increased demand on the health
care system as the number of older Americans grows will
create a crisis of unprecedented magnitude.

As C. Duane Dauner and Michael Bowker note in their
book *The Health Care Solution,*

> People over sixty-five years consume four times the health care
> services of people under sixty-five. People over eighty-five
> years consume twice as much health care as those between
> sixty-five and eighty-five. Moreover, their conditions are usu-
> ally chronic [ongoing] rather than episodic [self-limiting], re-
> quiring continuous, sometimes intensive care at greater cost.[27]

According to the federal Agency on Aging (AOA),
chronic health conditions measurably restrict daily living
for more than 53 percent of older Americans (those over
age sixty-five). Some of these conditions, such as os-
teoarthritis, are considered natural consequences of aging.
Others ailments, such as lung disease, are the result of
long-term lifestyle habits such as cigarette smoking.

Older Americans are also more likely to need urgent medical care for crisis conditions such as heart attacks and strokes, since the likelihood of such conditions increases with age. As a result, people over age sixty-five account for nearly 40 percent of the patients receiving hospital care, and they see the doctor more than twice as often as people under sixty-five. This imbalance causes concern among many within the health care industry, who fear the growing needs of older Americans will seriously strain health care resources.

Straining limited resources

America enjoys one of the most advanced health care systems in the world. Despite its flaws, it meets most of the nation's health care needs most of the time. Federal and state laws guarantee that no one will be denied lifesaving medical care, for example, and more than 80 percent of Americans have access to routine and preventive health care services.

The key to the availability of health care services is that not everyone needs care at the same time. While Americans

Many older Americans suffer chronic health problems, some brought on by longtime habits such as smoking.

make 750 billion trips to the doctor's office each year, they do not all go at once. In fact, 25 percent of Americans do not receive any health care services at all during the course of a year. Yet nearly 90 percent of those over age sixty-five see a doctor at least once a year, and many have multiple office visits because of chronic health conditions.

It is this disproportionately high percentage that worries some health care analysts. As the number of Americans over age sixty-five grows, so will their needs for health care services. The American health care system has evolved significantly over the past decades to accommodate the advances of technology and knowledge. Whether it can and will continue to accommodate increasing numbers of patients remains to be seen, however.

The Medicare crisis

Increasing demand for services is just one piece of the overall picture. Another key factor that affects the availability of health care resources is cost. In the years between 1940 and 1949, the United States spent about $400 million a year for health care. In the next decade, those costs tripled. Older Americans who were retired often had no means of paying for health care services since most health insurance plans were job benefits. To help them cope with such a rapid escalation of expenses, the U.S. Congress enacted the Medicare Act in 1966. The intent of this program, officially known as Title XVII of the Social Security Act, was to provide coverage for major medical expenses for every American age sixty-five and older.

In Medicare's first year, the average life expectancy in America was sixty-seven years for men and seventy-three years for women. There were just under 17 million Americans over the age of sixty-five. A little more than thirty years later, Medicare was the largest public payer for health care services. In 1996 it provided more than $200 billion in benefits for 38 million elderly and disabled Americans.

Working Americans support Medicare through a payroll tax. Employees and employers each pay half of the tax,

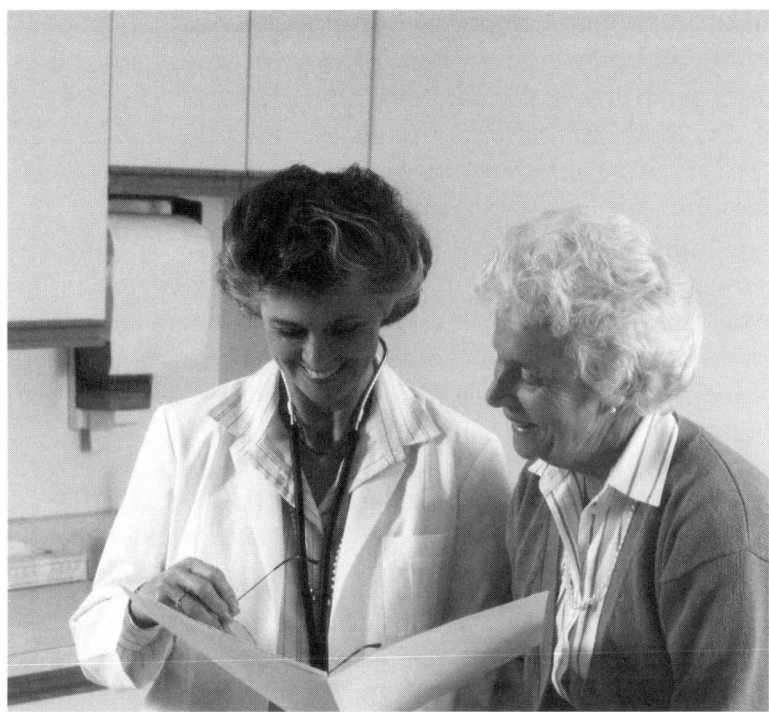

Millions of elderly Americans obtain health care through Medicare.

which goes into a trust fund. The money in the trust fund earns interest until it is used to pay for Medicare expenses. The fund relies on the premise that the contributions of those in the workforce today will pay for the health care needs of those currently enrolled in Medicare. When today's workers become eligible for Medicare, younger members of the workforce will be paying for their health care needs. With this "pass-through" method of funding, Medicare has enough money to pay current expenses but has no buffer for future ones.

Though Medicare benefits are generous, the program by no means covers everything. Basic Medicare, called Plan A, covers inpatient hospital care and skilled nursing care (short-term rehabilitation care in a nursing home). These are typically the most costly expenses in health care. Benefits have both financial and time limits. People enrolled in Medicare can also choose to purchase additional coverage, called Plan B, for doctor appointments, diagnostic tests, and outpatient care. Many services, including prescription drugs and routine physical examinations, are not covered by traditional Medicare, though they are often part of the coverage package for enrollees who chose to receive their care and benefits through a managed care plan.

Every American, whether working or retired, becomes eligible for Medicare Plan A on his or her sixty-fifth birthday. Since the number of people age sixty-five and over is growing, so too is the number of people receiving Medicare. As the number of people on Medicare increases, so do the program's costs. This has caused widespread concern that Medicare will run out of money—a concern that nearly became a reality in the 1980s.

Good intentions collide with economic reality

In 1988 it became clear that without radical changes, Medicare would be out of money in as little as a few months. There were too many people using too many services, and the program was paying out more than it was collecting in payroll taxes and trust-fund interest. Medicare, said lawmakers, was bleeding to death. Congress enacted a number of cost-controlling measures, including limitations on benefits, to stabilize Medicare funding. Congress also increased premiums and co-payments (the amount each person on Medicare pays).

Public officials soon realized that rising health care costs and increasing Medicare enrollment were not the only factors that were pushing Medicare toward bankruptcy. The funding crisis forced a close examination of Medicare billing and payment practices, which uncovered a serious problem with inaccurate and fraudulent claims. Most providers did the best they could to navigate what had become a complex sea of regulations and forms. A few providers took advantage of the confusion and intentionally overbilled Medicare patients. In 1996 Medicare paid more than $23 billion for erroneous billings—14 percent of all claims. Most of these bills were for unnecessary services (tests and procedures that made no difference in a person's diagnosis or treatment) or exaggerated the level of care that a person received.

"Good news, Mr. Ferguson, your insurance DOES cover needless surgery."

"The initial problem with Medicare when it came into being was that it encouraged cost excess in medicine," says family practice physician Mark Brooks. "There were incentives for people to be ill, not to remain well. People were put in the hospital for three or four days for a GI [gastrointestinal] work-up, for example, which is nothing more than a series of X rays."[28]

The federal government implemented administrative reforms and aggressive auditing procedures to reduce such losses. Congress passed the federal Balanced Budget Act of 1997, placing additional restrictions on services and payments. By 1998 Medicare had cut improper payments in half to $12.6 billion, or 7 percent of claims. Through these and other cost-control measures, the Medicare fund stabilized. Without further, and some say drastic, changes, however, the fund remains in danger of overextending once again. The number of people in the workforce whose taxes fund Medicare is steadily declining as the number of those enrolling in Medicare is increasing. When Medicare began in 1967, there were four employees to pay for each person on Medicare. In 1998 that number dropped to three. By 2030, when the last baby boomers retire, there will be only two employees for every Medicare recipient.

Though experts generally agree that Medicare must reduce its costs, there is little agreement about how this should take place. The challenge is to revise the Medicare system without jeopardizing health care coverage for the nearly 40 million Americans who rely on Medicare. Even with proposed budget cuts to reduce Medicare's operating expenses, the program still faces financial crisis. Analysts project that without significant reform, Medicare will run out of money by 2008.

Medicare reform efforts

Many organizations, ranging from the American Association of Retired Persons to the American Medical Association, have offered suggestions for revamping Medicare. Reform has become an important political issue as well, with every politician from congressional candidates to the president of the United States entering the discussion. Successful Medicare reform will require a careful balancing of needs and interests.

Many health care providers and analysts worry that older Americans, many of whom have paid into Medicare for decades, will end up bearing the brunt of Medicare reform efforts. Many proposals for controlling Medicare's costs incorporate some degree of cost sharing—that is, they require people on Medicare to pay more of their own health care expenses. Other proposals for reform recommend raising the minimum age at which people can enroll in Medicare. And still other proposals call for abandoning Medicare altogether.

Sharing costs

To cut costs and thus spend less, individuals may have to pay more for the health care services they use. Common methods for such cost sharing include higher deductibles and co-payments. Supporters of this approach say it's only

"NURSE, INCREASE MR. JOHNSON'S PAIN KILLER...I WANT TO SHOW HIM HIS BILL TODAY..."

fair for those who are using the services to pay a bigger share of their costs. This angers critics, who point out that of all segments of the American population, the elderly are the least able to pay more for anything. They also note that despite Medicare's high costs, seniors on Medicare already are finding themselves responsible for paying more services on their own.

According to the Agency for Health Care Policy and Research, the average American over age sixty-five already spends 14 percent of his or her personal income on health care; people under age sixty-five only spend 7 percent. Most retirees receive monthly pensions or Social Security (the federal government's public retirement program). For Americans who depend on Social Security, an increase in the costs of health care can mean choosing between medications and other essentials such as food or rent.

Some reform proposals attempt to soften the blow of higher costs by offering additional benefits such as limited

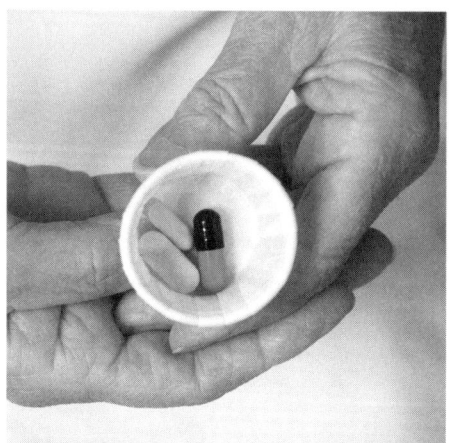

Under some reform proposals, Medicare would offer limited coverage for prescription drugs.

coverage for prescription drugs and other services traditionally not covered by Medicare. A major criticism of the current Medicare program is that it does not cover the services the elderly use the most, particularly prescription drugs. Proposals that expand benefits are often popular with both retirees and providers. However, some analysts question whether this approach solves any of Medicare's long-term problems and whether expanding benefits is really necessary. Most retirees who can afford to do so purchase "medigap" insurance already, to offset Medicare's shortcomings. Such insurance policies pick up many of the expenses that are not covered by Medicare. Many people who cannot afford medigap insurance are likely to qualify for Medicaid, the public insurance program for low-income individuals. Adding benefits to Medicare helps only those in the middle—who make too much to qualify for Medicaid but not enough to pay for private insurance—and their numbers are dwindling.

Another way to increase the individual's share of the costs is through premiums—regular payments made whether or not the person used any health care services. Those who participate in Medicare Plan B, which provides coverage for doctors' visits and other outpatient services, already pay a premium for the additional benefits. Most premium proposals suggest a sliding scale, with those at lower income levels paying less than those at higher income levels. People who oppose extending premiums to basic Medicare (Plan A) fear that those who are in relatively good health would choose not to enroll in Medicare, waiting until they anticipated health needs. This defeats the intent of premiums, which is to spread the costs across a wide pool of healthy as well as not so healthy individuals. There is also some concern that elderly individuals who no longer manage their personal affairs consistently could lose track of the need to pay and end up dropped from coverage.

Still other cost-sharing proposals target providers by suggesting reduced reimbursements. Doctors and hospitals strongly oppose such recommendations, protesting that Medicare payments are already well below cost for most services. This has become such a flashpoint that every year more HMOs across the country withdraw from Medicare. In 1998 such withdrawals left three hundred thousand people on Medicare in eighteen states scrambling to find new doctors. HMOs, which often agree to accept a flat payment for each Medicare member, say they cannot provide the services that such members need at the rates the government wants to pay.

And some experts recommend shifting costs in another direction—back to the employees who pay for Medicare through payroll taxes. Increasing those taxes would bring more money into the Medicare trust fund. With more money, they reason, Medicare could pay for the increased demands of its growing enrollment. Not surprisingly, both employees and employers strongly oppose this recommendation. In 1999 every employer and employee paid 1.5 percent in taxes to support Medicare, an amount often more than the cost of premiums for the employee's own health insurance. Critics of this option also note that throwing more money at Medicare's problems will not make them go away. Key issues such as inefficiency will continue to drain the fund, no matter how much money is there.

Changing eligibility

The present Medicare program is available to all Americans who turn sixty-five, despite whether they are retired or are still working. Even seniors who have never worked are eligible. In this way, Medicare is an entitlement program—once an individual passes age sixty-five, he or she is entitled to Medicare benefits without further qualifications. Many health care policy analysts feel that this is unfair. A good number of retirees are financially well off, if not wealthy, yet they receive the same public support as do those who have very limited resources. Some experts recommend adding eligibility requirements that consider an individual's financial situation and possibly his or her working status. Such a "means test" would determine whether a person had the resources to pay a greater portion of his or her health coverage. In general, the well-to-do would pay more for their Medicare benefits than those at low income levels, though all would receive the same coverage.

Other eligibility proposals look at changing the minimum age for Medicare from sixty-five to sixty-seven or even seventy, based on increasing life expectancies and later retirements. Without other changes, however, these proposals only postpone the wave of baby boomers headed for retirement. Raising the age limit for Medicare does nothing to change the way the program operates.

Ending Medicare

President Johnson signs legislation authorizing the start of Medicare.

Some analysts advocate ending Medicare as it has traditionally existed. They point out that Medicare was never intended to be the blanket of medical coverage that it has become. When President Lyndon Johnson signed Medicare

into existence in 1966, retired Americans had few resources to pay for their health care needs. Forty years earlier, when those retirees entered the workforce, medical care was basic at best. People went to a doctor when there was no other option, and they went to a hospital to die. While employees in the 1950s and 1960s were beginning to set up retirement pensions that included some structure for health care needs, those who were retiring then had not done so.

Thirty years later, the situation had become very different. In 1996 nearly 70 percent of Americans under age sixty-five had private health insurance, which is often sponsored by their employers, to pay for their medical needs. Yet nearly 100 percent of those age sixty-five and older were on Medicare, even if they were still working. Today more people are staying on the job past the former retirement age of sixty-five. However, once an employee turns sixty-five, he or she becomes eligible for Medicare and is then excluded from receiving private health insurance coverage.

Some analysts recommend changing this to allow anyone who is working, regardless of age, to choose private health insurance instead of Medicare. The insurance industry objects to this suggestion. Because older people use more health care services than younger people, say industry representatives, including them in private insurance plans would cause costs to go up for everyone.

A closely related option would be to privatize Medicare, meaning the government would contract with private health care providers for all services. One form of this is an approach called defined contribution. As one analyst explains, this would "move Medicare away from offering a guaranteed insurance benefit for those eligible for the program and instead establish a fixed contribution toward the cost of health insurance for those beneficiaries."[29]

Since the private health care market is competitive, supporters believe this could result in a natural decrease in costs as providers themselves strive to hold down expenses. If health care expenses continue to rise, however, insurers might reduce benefits or pass costs on to Medicare members through increased co-payments. To succeed, this option would require a certain level of government oversight to assure consistent services and costs. This would ultimately be little different than the current system.

An uncertain future

There are many variables that influence the health of Medicare. Most social programs flourish when the general economy is strong and struggle when it slumps. There is no way to predict what the economic environment will be five or ten years into the future. Nor is there any way to

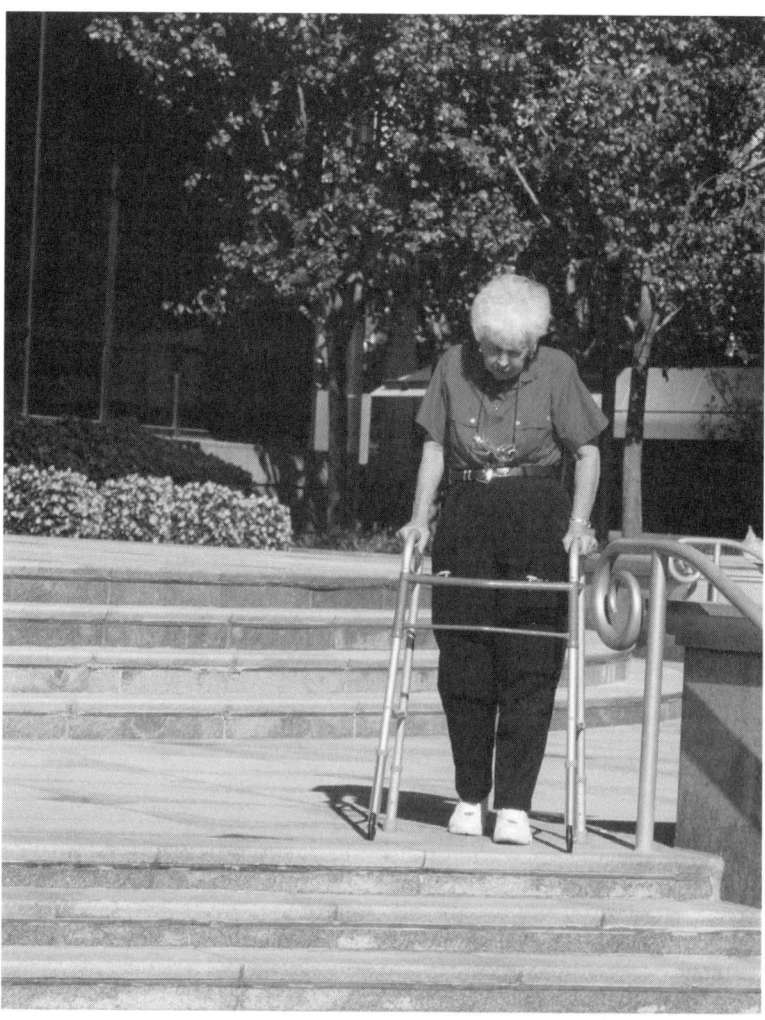

Economic and population trends may influence the future of Medicare—and health care in general.

know what medical discoveries are just beyond the horizon. Though the baby boom generation has forced the issue of Medicare reform, there are no clear-cut solutions to current and potential problems. It is fairly certain, however, that any successful restructuring of Medicare will have to incorporate ideas from many of the various reform proposals.

Notes

Chapter 1: Managing Health Care

1. C. Duane Dauner with Michael Bowker, *The Health Care Solution: Understanding the Crisis and the Cure.* Sacramento: Vision, 1994, p. 17.

2. Dauner and Bowker, *The Health Care Solution,* p. 34.

3. Mark Brooks, interview with the author, October 2, 1998.

4. Brooks, interview with the author.

5. Quoted in James D. Torr, ed., *Health Care: Opposing Viewpoints.* San Diego: Greenhaven, 2000, p. 65.

6. Quoted in Torr, *Health Care,* p. 94.

7. Quoted in Torr, *Health Care,* p. 94.

8. Quoted in Torr, *Health Care,* p. 94.

9. Brooks, interview with the author.

10. Ruth Shuck, interview with the author, August 20, 1998.

11. Bill Ainsworth, "Governor Signs Major HMO Reforms," *San Diego Union-Tribune,* September 28, 1999, p. A1.

Chapter 2: Rationing Health Care

12. Quoted in *Jackson Clarion-Ledger,* "David Crosby Gets New Liver After Surgery," November 21, 1994. www.geoclio.st.usm.edu/~dadunn/crozop.html.

13. Andrew Glass, interview with the author, September 1, 1998.

14. Quoted in Carol Wekesser, ed., *Health Care in America: Opposing Viewpoints.* San Diego: Greenhaven, 1994, pp. 192–93.

15. Quoted in Torr, *Health Care,* p. 52.

Chapter 3: Keeping Communities Healthy

16. Quoted in Reuters Health, "Poor Diet Sends Obesity Rates Soaring in California," September 24, 1999. www.dailynews.yahoo.com/h/nm/19990924/hl/ca15_1.html.

17. U.S. Department of Health and Human Services, Office of Disease Prevention and Health Promotion, Healthy People 2000 fact sheet. www.odphp.osophs.dhhs.gov/pubs/hp2000/hp2kfact.htm.

Chapter 4: The Doctor Shortage in Rural America

18. Quoted in Michael Romano, "Shortage of Physicians in Rural Areas Unlikely to Be Filled Anytime Soon," *Denver Rocky Mountain News,* April 21, 1996, p. 6A.

19. Quoted in Romano, "Shortage of Physicians," p. 6A.

20. Quoted in *Health Care News Server*, "Physician Workforce Recommendations Endorsed by ACP," January 20, 1998. www.healthcarenewsserver.com/stories/HCN1998000004.shtml.

21. Walter M. Swentko, interview with the author, August 27, 1998.

22. Swentko, interview with the author.

23. Quoted in Jim Angle, "International Doctors Fill Void in Rural U.S.," *CNN Interactive,* May 25, 1996.

24. Quoted in Angle, "International Doctors Fill Void in Rural U.S."

25. *JAMA Online,* "Physicians Put Promise of Telemedicine to the Test: Reports from Rural Practitioners, Anesthesiologists," July 24–31, 1996. www.ama-assn.org/sci-pubs/journals/archive/jama/vol_276/no_4/mn6129.htm.

26. Quoted in Romano, "Shortage of Physicians," p. 6A.

Chapter 5: Caring for an Aging Population

27. Dauner and Bowker, *The Health Care Solution,* p. 14.

28. Brooks, interview with the author.

29. Marilyn Moon, "Restructuring Medicare: Impacts on Beneficiaries," Urban Institute, January 1999. www.urban.org/health/medicare_restructuring.html.

Organizations to Contact

Agency for Health Care Policy and Research (AHCPR)
Executive Office Center, Suite 600
2101 E. Jefferson St.
Rockville, MD 20852
(301) 594-6662
website: www.ahcpr.gov
A part of the U.S. Department of Health and Human Services, the AHCPR supports research designed to improve the quality of health care, reduce its cost, and broaden access to essential services. The agency emphasizes practical, science-based information for physicians and consumers.

Alan Guttmacher Institute (AGI)
120 Wall St.
New York, NY 10005
(212) 248-1111
website: www.agi-usa.org

The Alan Guttmacher Institute (AGI) studies and reports on reproductive health issues worldwide. The website features many articles about pregnancy, contraception, and related topics. Articles provide in-depth analysis and statistics. AGI staff respond promptly to e-mail inquiries for more information about AGI projects and reports.

American Academy of Family Physicians (AAFP)
8880 Ward Pkwy.
Kansas City, MO 64114
(816) 333-9700
website: www.aafp.org
The AAFP website provides a wide variety of statistical information about family physicians in America, including a series of summary tables called "Facts About Family Practice."

American Demographics
PO Box 10580
Riverton, NJ 08076-0580
(800) 529-7502
website: www.demographics.com

American Demographics posts extensive articles about consumer trends and related business information on its website. Articles reference sources and source data. The website includes good links to government and private websites that provide related information. *American Demographics Magazine* is available for review online and in a print version by subscription.

Centers for Disease Control and Prevention (CDC)
National Center for Health Statistics (NCHS)
6525 Belcrest Rd.
Hyattsville, MD 20782-2003
(301) 436-8500
website: www.cdc.gov/nchswww

The NCHS is the primary federal organization that collects, analyzes, and distributes a wide range of health statistics. The FASTATS section (also called the Statistical Rolodex) of its website contains summary reports for the most current data.

Health Care Financing Administration
website: www.hcfa.gov

An agency of the U.S. Department of Health and Human Services, the Health Care Financing Administration runs the Medicare and Medicaid programs and the Children's Health Insurance Program.

National Center for Policy Analysis (NCPA)
655 15th St. NW, Suite 375
Washington, DC 20005
(202) 628-6671
website: www.ncpa.org

The NCPA's website has statistics for and analyses of many aspects of health care in America. Articles cite original sources.

National Coalition on Health Care

website: www.nchc.org

The National Coalition on Health Care is the nation's largest and most broadly representative alliance working to improve America's health care system. Its members include nonprofit and nonpartisan groups that believe Americans need and should have better, more affordable health care.

Robert Wood Johnson Foundation

Route 1 and College Rd. East
PO Box 2316
Princeton, NJ 08543-2316
website: www.rwjf.org

The Robert Wood Johnson Foundation strives to improve the health and health care of all Americans. It funds grants to support research in the key areas of access to care, substance abuse, and chronic care.

University of Minnesota
Rural Physician Associate Program

5-255 PWB
516 Delaware SE
Minneapolis, MN 55455
(612) 624-3111 • (800) 665-7727
www.rpap.umn.edu

The Rural Physician Associate Program, the country's first physician training program in rural medicine, hosts a website that provides information about rural medicine and the University of Minnesota's revolutionary program.

U.S. Department of Health and Human Services

200 Independence Ave. SW
Washington, DC 20201
(202) 619-0257 • (877) 696-6775
 website: www.os.dhhs.gov

The Department of Health and Human Services is the primary agency that protects the health of Americans. It provides essential health and social services, especially for those who are least able to help themselves.

Suggestions for Further Reading

Janice Castro, *The American Way of Health: How Medicine Is Changing and What It Means to You*. Boston: Little, Brown, 1994. Discusses how health care used to be, why it has changed, and how it has changed.

Nancy Levitin, *America's Health Care Crisis: Who's Responsible?* New York: Franklin Watts, 1994. Explains how the various components of America's health care system have contributed to the cost and resource crisis of the 1980s and 1990s.

James D. Torr, ed., *Health Care: Opposing Viewpoints*. San Diego: Greenhaven, 2000. An anthology that provides viewpoints on health care issues ranging from managed care to reforming the health care system.

Carol Wekesser, ed., *Health Care in America: Opposing Viewpoints*. San Diego: Greenhaven Press, 1994. An anthology of articles written by various experts that discusses key health care issues.

Lisa Yount, *Issues in Biomedical Ethics*. San Diego: Lucent Books, 1998. Provides in-depth discussion of ethical concerns and decisions in modern health care.

Works Consulted

Books

George Anders, *Health Against Wealth: HMOs and the Breakdown of Medical Trust.* New York: Houghton Mifflin, 1996. This Wall Street reporter examines how the desire to make money has influenced changes in the health care industry.

Edward R. Annis, *Code Blue: Health Care in Crisis.* Washington, DC: Regnery Gateway, 1993. This book examines the factors that have come together to create a state of crisis in the American health care system.

C. Duane Dauner with Michael Bowker, *The Health Care Solution: Understanding the Crisis and the Cure.* Sacramento: Vision, 1994. This book focuses on the role of market economics in the health care industry.

Jane M. Orient, *Your Doctor Is Not In: Healthy Skepticism About National Health Care.* New York: Crown, 1994. The author provides an "inside" view of the American health care system and the issues that confront doctors.

Marc J. Roberts with Alexandra T. Clyde, *Your Money or Your Life: The Health Care Crisis Explained.* New York: Main Street Books/Doubleday, 1993. This book explores the relationship between a person's ability to pay and the health care services he or she receives.

U.S. Domestic Policy Council, *The President's Health Security Plan: The Complete Draft and Final Reports of the White House Domestic Policy Council.* New York: Times Books, 1993. This is the full text of President Bill Clinton's health care reform proposal as it was presented to the U.S. Congress.

Periodicals

Bill Ainsworth, "Governor Signs Major HMO Reforms,"
San Diego Union-Tribune, September 28, 1999.

Eric Anderson, "Limousine Medicine: When Is It Time to
Hit the Brakes?" *American Medical News,* July 21, 1997.

Jim Angle, "International Doctors Fill Void in Rural U.S.,"
CNN Interactive, May 25, 1996.

Peter P. Budetti, "Health Care Reform for the Twenty-First
Century? It May Have to Wait Until the Twenty-First Century,"
JAMA, January 15, 1997.

Paul Hammel, "Troubled Doctors See Rural Areas as
Second Chance," *Omaha World Herald,* August 21, 1994.

Robert Pear, "HMO to Cut Thousands of Medicare Enrollees,"
Tacoma News Tribune, October 2, 1998.

Karie Praszek et al., "Family Medicine: A Call to the Front
Line," *JAMA,* May 6, 1998.

Michael Romano, "Shortage of Physicians in Rural Areas
Unlikely to Be Filled Anytime Soon," *Denver Rocky Mountain
News,* April 21, 1996.

Internet Sources

Administration on Aging, "Protected Health Conditions
Among the Elderly." www.aoa.dhhs.gov/aoa/stats/aging21/
health.html.

Agency for Health Care Policy Research, "Access to Care:
Millions Face Obstacles in Accessing Medical Care." www.
ahcpr.gov/research/nov97/ra2.htm.

———, "Health Care Use in America—1996," May 1999.
www.meps.ahcpr.gov/papers/99-0029/99-0029.htm.

———, "Health Insurance Coverage in America—1996."
www.meps.ahcpr.gov/papers/98-0031/98-0031v3a.htm.

———, "Research in Action: Improving Health Care for
Rural Populations." www.ahcpr.gov/research/rural.htm.

Kim Barker, "Covington Man Receives Stem-Cell Transplant," *Seattle Times,* March 23, 1999. www.seattletimes.com/news/local/html98/stem_19990323.html.

Charles Bierbauer, "Doctors and Managed Care—Are HMOs Good Medicine?" *CNN Interactive,* July 15, 1998. www.cnn.com/HEALTH/9807/15/hmo.docs.prognosis/html.

Robert C. Bowman, "Continuing Family Medicine's Unique Contribution to Rural Health Care," *American Family Physician,* August 1996. www.aafp.org/afp/080196/med-soc.html.

John Clark, "Rural Medicine Goes High Tech," *Nevada Appeal,* March 5, 1998. www.tahoe.com/appeal/stories.3.5.98/news/a1ruralhealt05Mar1895.html.

John Dickerson, "Who Will Swallow Medicare's Bitter Pills?" *Time Online,* July 5, 1999. www.pathfinder.com/time/magazine/articles/0,3266,27445,00.html.

Brad Edmondson, "Where There Is No Doctor," *American Demographics Online,* March 1996. www.demographics.com/publications/ad/96_ad/9603_ad/9603ad06.htm.

Electronic Policy Network, "Facts on . . . Medicare: Hospital Insurance and Supplementary Medical Insurance." www.epn.org/library/agmedi.html.

Steve Fox, "Medicare: The Issue," *Washington Post,* May 5, 1999. www.washingtonpost.com/wp-srv/politics/special/medicare/issue.html.

———, "Medicare: State of Play," *Washington Post,* May 5, 1999. www.washingtonpost.com/wp-srv/politics/special/medicare/issue.html.

Thomas Gavagan and Lisa Brodyaga, "Medical Care for Immigrants and Refugees," *American Family Physician,* March 1, 1998. www.aafp.org/980301ap/gavagan.html.

The Guttmacher Report, "Falling Teen Pregnancy, Birth Rates: What's Behind the Decline?" Alan Guttmacher Institute, October 1998. www.agi-usa.org/pubs/journals/gr010506.html.

———, "U.S. Teenage Pregnancy Rate Now Lowest in Two Decades," Alan Guttmacher Institute, 1998. www.agi-usa.org/pubs/archives/grnr0105.html.

Health Care Financing Administration, "Highlights of the National Health Expenditure Projections, 1997–2007." www.hcfa.gov/stats/nhe-proj/hilites.htm.

Health Care News Server, "Physician Workforce Recommendations Endorsed by ACP," January 20, 1998. www.healthcarenewsserver.com/stories/ HCN1998000004.shmtl.

Tim Hepher, "UN Says Global Hunger Easing But Sees Shortfall," *Reuters,* November 13, 1999. www.dailynews.yahoo.com.

Bob Herzog, "The Magnificent Seven: Mickey Mantle, the Legendary Yankee Slugger, Was Both an American Hero and Tragic Figure," *Newsday,* August 14, 1995. www.newsday.com/yankees/micksp4.htm.

Martha Irvine, "Dr.'s Diploma Doesn't Guarantee Job," Associated Press, September 1, 1998. www.dailynews.yahoo.com/headlines/ap/us/story.html.

Jackson Clarion-Ledger, "David Crosby Gets New Liver After Surgery," November 21, 1994. www.geoclio.st.usm.edu/~dadunn/crozop.html.

JAMA Online, "Physicians Put Promise of Telemedicine to the Test: Reports from Rural Practitioners, Anesthesiologists," July 24–31, 1996. www.ama-assn.org/sci-pubs/journals/archive/jama/vol_276/no_4/mn6129.htm.

———, "Science News Update: Medical School Program Increases Supply of Physicians in Rural Areas," January 20, 1999. www.ama-assn.org/sci-pubs/sci-news/1999/snr0120.htm.

John Keilman, "Hurting for Physicians," *Dayton Daily News,* February 21, 1999. www.activedayton.com/news/1999/02/21/physicians.html.

Will Lester, "Survey: Most Say No on Living to One Hundred," Associated Press, May 25, 1999. www.dailynews.yahoo.com.

Merritt McKinney, "Being Overweight Increases Risk of Death," Reuters Health, October 6, 1999. www.dailynews.yahoo.com/h/n/nm/19991006/hl/bmi10_1.html.

MMWR Weekly, "Health-Related Quality of Life and Activity Limitation—Eight States, 1995," February 27, 1998, Centers for Disease Control. www.cdc.gov/eop/mmwr/preview/mmwrhtml/00051443.htm.

Marilyn Moon, "Restructuring Medicare: Impacts on Beneficiaries," Urban Institute, January 1999. www.urban.org/health/medicare_restructuring.html.

Geir Moulson, "AIDS Is Top Infectious Killer," Associated Press, May 11, 1999. www.dailynews.yahoo.com.

National Maternal and Child Clearinghouse, "Healthy Start Facts About Infant Mortality." www.mchb.hrsa.gov/healthys.htm.

Reuters Health, "Poor Diet Sends Obesity Rates Soaring in California," September 24, 1999. www.dailynews.yahoo.com/h/nm/19990924/hl/cal5_1.html.

C. G. Schenck-Yglesias, "How Many Doctors Does It Take?" *American Demographics Online,* April 1995. www.demographics.com.

Bill Stoneman, "Is There a Doctor in the State?" *American Demographics Online,* July 1997. www.demographics.com/publications/ad/97_ad/9707_ad/ad970719.htm.

———, "This May Hurt," *American Demographics Online,* July 1997. www.demographics.com/publications/ad/97_ad/9707_ad/ad970718.htm.

UNICEF, "Malnutrition in Industrialized Countries," *State of the World's Children.* www.unicef.org/sowc98/.

U.S. Census Bureau, "Sixty-Five Plus in the United States," Report P23-190. www.census.gov/prod/1/pop/p23-190/p23-190.html.

U.S. Department of Health and Human Services, Office of Disease Prevention and Health Promotion, Healthy People

2000 fact sheet. www.odphp.osophs.dhhs.gov/pubs/hp2000/hp2kfact.htm.

Robin M. Weinick, Samuel H. Zuvekas, and Susan Drilea, "Access to Health Care—Sources and Barriers, 1996," Agency for Health Care Policy and Research. www.meps.ahcpr.gov/highlit/find3/rf3text.htm.

Index

University of Minnesota, 52
unnecessary medical
 procedures, 15
UNOS. *See* United Network
 for Organ Sharing
U.S. News & World Report, 18

Village Voice (newspaper), 35

walking, 41
Washington (state), 23
whooping cough, 37

Picture Credits

Cover Photo: PhotoDisc
AFP/Corbis, 10
AP/Wide World Photos, 32
Bettmann/Corbis, 9, 60, 70
Corbis, 68
Fotografia, Inc./Corbis, 63
Owen Franken/Corbis, 18
Annie Griffiths Belt/Corbis, 45
Julie Houck/Corbis, 51
Impact Visuals, 25
Impact Visuals/Earl Dotter, 43
Dan Lamont/Corbis, 39
Buddy Mays/Corbis, 61
Hank Morgan/Science Source/Photo Researchers, Inc., 47
PhotoDisc, 15, 20, 31, 34, 35, 38, 41, 53, 55, 57, 72
Photo Researchers, Inc., 50
Vittoriano Rastelli/Corbis, 28
Roger Ressmeyer/Corbis, 13
USDA, 40

About the Author

Deborah S. Romaine has published eight books, more than three hundred articles, and a half-dozen short stories. She has worked in the health care industry for fifteen years and has done considerable writing about health care topics. Ms. Romaine has an M.A. degree in English and creative writing from the University of Washington and teaches classes in creative writing. She enjoys bicycling, camping, and fishing in the spectacular Pacific Northwest, where she lives with her husband and two children.